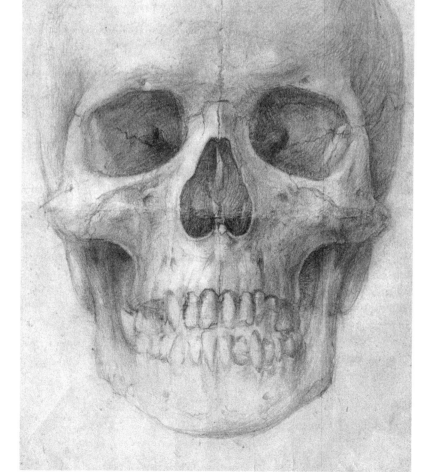

COMBAT
PRESSURE POINTS

by
Sammy Franco

Also by Sammy Franco

Knife Fighting
Knock Out
Survival Weapons
Cane Fighting
Double End Bag Training
The Heavy Bag Bible
The Widow Maker Compendium
Invincible: Mental Toughness Techniques for Peak Performance
Unleash Hell: A Step-by-Step Guide to Devastating Widow Maker Combinations
Feral Fighting: Advanced Widow Maker Fighting Techniques
The Widow Maker Program: Extreme Self-Defense for Deadly Force Situations
Savage Street Fighting: Tactical Savagery as a Last Resort
Heavy Bag Workout
Heavy Bag Combinations
Heavy Bag Training
The Complete Body Opponent Bag Book
Stand and Deliver: A Street Warrior's Guide to Tactical Combat Stances
Maximum Damage: Hidden Secrets Behind Brutal Fighting Combinations
First Strike: End a Fight in Ten Seconds or Less!
The Bigger They Are, The Harder They Fall
Self-Defense Tips and Tricks
Kubotan Power: Quick & Simple Steps to Mastering the Kubotan Keychain
Gun Safety: For Home Defense and Concealed Carry
Out of the Cage: A Guide to Beating a Mixed Martial Artist on the Street
Warrior Wisdom: Inspiring Ideas from the World's Greatest Warriors
War Machine: How to Transform Yourself Into a Vicious Street Fighter
1001 Street Fighting Secrets
When Seconds Count: Self-Defense for the Real World
Killer Instinct: Unarmed Combat for Street Survival
Street Lethal: Unarmed Urban Combat

Combat Pressure Points
Copyright © 2022 by Sammy Franco
ISBN: 978-1-941845-67-7
Printed in the United States of America
Visit online at: ContemporaryFightingArts.com

For Amy

Contents

"No pressure, no diamonds."

– Thomas Carlyle

Disclaimer

The author, publisher, and distributors of this book disclaim any liability from loss, injury, or damage, personal or otherwise, resulting from the information and procedures in this book. This book is for academic study only.

The information contained in this book is not designed to diagnose, treat, or manage any physical health conditions.

Before you begin any exercise or activity, including those suggested in this book, it is important to check with your physician to see if you have any condition that might be aggravated by strenuous training.

About this Book

Combat Pressure Points is a concise guide designed to teach you some of the most practical and effective pressure point fighting techniques for real world self-defense.

The skills featured in this book are simple and can be readily used by young and old, regardless of size or strength and level of experience. Most importantly, you don't need martial arts training to apply many of these devastating fighting techniques.

Unlike other pressure point books, this book is devoid of impractical and gimmicky techniques that can get you injured or possibly killed when faced with a real-world self-defense crisis. Instead, this book arms you with the most efficient, effective, and practical pressure point strikes that work in the chaos of a real-world survival situation. In fact, the self-defense skills and techniques found within these pages are straightforward and easy to apply.

Practitioners who regularly practice the pressure point skills featured in this book will establish a rock solid foundation for using them in self-defense. Moreover, the techniques featured in this book will significantly improve your overall personal protection skills, enhance your conditioning, and introduce you to an exciting method of self-defense.

Combat Pressure Points is based on my 30+ years of research, training and teaching reality-based self-defense and combat sciences. In fact, I've taught these unique fighting skills to thousands of my students, and I'm confident they can help protect you and your loved ones during an emergency self-defense situation.

I also encourage you to read this book from beginning to end, chapter by chapter. Only after you have read the entire book should you treat it as a reference and skip around, reading those chapters that directly apply to you

Finally, the information, techniques, and suggestions contained herein are dangerous and should only be used to protect yourself or a loved one from the immediate risk of unlawful injury.

Remember, the decision to use physical force for self-defense must always be a last resort, after all other means of avoiding violence have been exhausted.

Walk in peace!

Sammy Franco

Introduction
Contemporary Fighting Arts

A State-Of-The-Art Combat System

Before diving into this book, I'd like to first introduce you to my unique system of combat, Contemporary Fighting Arts (CFA). I hope it will give you a greater appreciation of the material covered in this book. For those of you already familiar with CFA, you can skip to chapter one.

Contemporary Fighting Arts® (CFA), is a state-of-the-art self-defense system that was originally introduced to the world in 1983. This sophisticated and practical system of self-defense is designed specifically to provide efficient and effective methods to avoid, defuse, confront, and neutralize both armed and unarmed assailants in a variety of deadly situations and circumstances.

Unlike karate, kung-fu, mixed martial arts and the like, CFA is the first offensive-based American martial art that is specifically designed for the violence that plagues our cruel city streets. CFA dispenses with the extraneous and the impractical and focuses on real-life street fighting.

Every tool, technique and tactic found within the CFA system must meet three essential criteria for fighting: efficiency, effectiveness, and safety. Efficiency means that the techniques permit you to reach your combative objective quickly and economically. Effectiveness means that the elements of the system will produce the desired effect. Finally, Safety means that the combative elements provide the least amount of danger and risk for you - the fighter.

CFA is not about mind-numbing tournaments or senseless competition. It does not require you to waste time and energy practicing forms (katas) or other impractical rituals. There are

3

no theatrical kicks or exotic techniques. Finally, CFA does not adhere blindly to tradition for tradition's sake. Simply put, it is a scientific yet pragmatic approach to staying alive on the streets.

CFA has been taught to people of all walks of life. Some include the U.S. Border Patrol, police officers, deputy sheriffs, security guards, military personnel, private investigators, surgeons, lawyers, college professors, airline pilots, as well as black belts, boxers, and kick boxers. CFA's broad appeal results from its ability to teach people how to really fight.

It's All In The Name!

Before discussing the three components that make up Contemporary Fighting Arts, it is important to understand how CFA acquired its unique name. To begin, the first word, "Contemporary," was selected because it refers to the system's modern, up-to-date orientation. Unlike traditional martial arts, CFA is specifically designed to meet the challenges of our modern world.

4

The second term, "Fighting," was chosen because it accurately describes the system's combat orientation. After all, why not just call it Contemporary Martial Arts? There are two reasons for this. First, the word "martial" conjures up images of traditional and impractical martial art forms that are antithetical to the system. Second, why dilute a perfectly functional name when the word "fighting" defines the system so succinctly? Contemporary Fighting Arts is about teaching people how to really fight.

Let's look at the last word, "Arts." In the subjective sense, "art" refers to the combat skills that are acquired through arduous study, practice, and observation. The bottom line is that effective street fighting skills will require consistent practice and attention. Take, for example, something as seemingly basic as an elbow strike, which will actually require hundreds of hours of practice to perfect.

The pluralization of the word "Art" reflects CFA's protean instruction. The various components of CFA's training (i.e., firearms training, stick fighting, ground fighting, natural body weapon mastery, and so on) have all truly earned their status as individual art forms and, as such, require years of consistent study and practice to perfect.

To acquire a greater understanding of CFA, here is an overview of the system's three vital components: the physical, the mental, and the spiritual.

The Physical Component

The physical component of CFA focuses on the physical development of a fighter, including physical fitness, weapon and technique mastery, and self-defense attributes.

5

Physical Fitness

If you are going to prevail in a street fight, you must be physically fit. It's that simple. In fact, you will never master the tools and skills of combat unless you're in excellent physical shape. On the average, you will have to spend more than an hour a day to achieve maximum fitness.

In CFA physical fitness comprises the following three broad components: cardiorespiratory conditioning, muscular/skeletal conditioning, and proper body composition.

The cardiorespiratory system includes the heart, lungs, and circulatory system, which undergo tremendous stress during the course of a street fight. So you're going to have to run, jog, bike, swim, or skip rope to develop sound cardiorespiratory conditioning. Each aerobic workout should last a minimum of 30 minutes and be performed at least four times per week.

The second component of physical fitness is muscular/skeletal conditioning. In the streets, the strong survive and the rest go to the morgue. To strengthen your bones and muscles to withstand the rigors of a real fight, your program must include progressive resistance (weight training) and calisthenics. You will also need a stretching program designed to loosen up every muscle group. You can't kick, punch, ground fight, or otherwise execute the necessary body mechanics if you're "tight" or inflexible. Stretching on a regular basis will also increase the muscles' range of motion, improve circulation, reduce the possibility of injury, and relieve daily stress.

The final component of physical fitness is proper body composition: simply, the ratio of fat to lean body tissue. Your diet and training regimen will affect your level or percentage of body fat significantly. A sensible and consistent exercise program accompanied by a healthy and balanced diet will facilitate proper body composition. Do not neglect this important aspect of physical fitness.

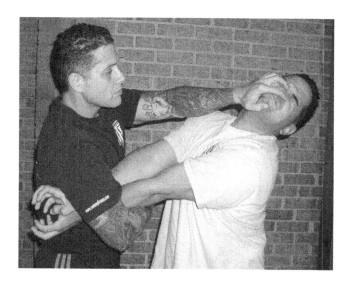

Weapon and Technique Mastery

You won't stand a chance against a vicious assailant if you don't master the weapons and tools of fighting. In CFA, we teach our students both armed and unarmed methods of combat. Unarmed fighting requires that you master a complete arsenal of natural body weapons and techniques. In conjunction, you must also learn the various stances, hand positioning, footwork, body mechanics, defensive structure, locks, chokes, and various holds. Keep in mind that something as simple as a basic punch will actually require hundreds of hours to perfect.

Range proficiency is another important aspect of weapon and technique mastery. Briefly, range proficiency is the ability to fight effectively in all three ranges of unarmed fighting. Although punching range tools are emphasized in CFA, kicking and grappling ranges cannot be neglected. Our kicking range tools consist of deceptive and powerful low-line kicks. Grappling range tools include head-butts, elbows, knees, foot stomps, biting, tearing, gouging, and crushing tactics.

Although CFA focuses on striking, we also teach our students a myriad of chokes, locks, and holds that can be used in a ground fight. While such grappling range submission techniques are not the most preferred methods of dealing with a ground fighting situation, they must be studied for the following six reasons:

(1) level of force - many ground fighting situations do not justify the use of deadly force. In such instances, you must apply various non-lethal submission holds.

(2) nature of the beast - in order to escape any choke, lock or hold, you must first know how to apply them yourself.

(3) occupational requirement- some professional occupations (police, security, etc.) require that you possess a

working knowledge of various submission techniques.

(4) subduing a friend or relative - in many cases it is best to restrain and control a friend or relative with a submission hold instead of striking him with a natural body weapon.

(5) anatomical orientation - practicing various chokes, locks and holds will help you develop a strong orientation of the human anatomy.

(6) refutation requirement - finally, if you are going to criticize the combative limitations of any submission hold, you better be sure that you can perform it yourself.

Defensive tools and skills are also taught. Our defensive structure is efficient, uncomplicated, and impenetrable. It provides the fighter maximum protection while allowing complete freedom of choice for acquiring offensive control. Our defensive structure is based on distance, parrying, blocking, evading, mobility, and stance structure. Simplicity is always the key.

Students are also instructed in specific methods of armed

fighting. For example, CFA provides instruction about firearms for personal and household protection. We provide specific guidelines for handgun purchasing, operation, nomenclature, proper caliber, shooting fundamentals, cleaning, and safe storage. Our firearm program also focuses on owner responsibility and the legal ramifications regarding the use of deadly force.

CFA's weapons program also consists of natural body weapons, knives and edged weapons, single and double stick, makeshift weaponry, the side-handle baton, and oleoresin capsicum (OC) spray.

Combat Attributes

Your offensive and defensive tools are useless unless they are used strategically. For any tool or technique to be effective in a real fight, it must be accompanied by specific attributes. Attributes are qualities that enhance a particular tool, technique, or maneuver. Some examples include speed, power, timing, coordination, accuracy, non-telegraphic movement, balance, and target orientation.

CFA also has a wide variety of training drills and methodologies designed to develop and sharpen these combat attributes. For example, our students learn to ground fight while blindfolded, spar with one arm tied down, and fight while handcuffed.

Reality is the key. For example, in class students participate in full-contact exercises against fully padded assailants, and real weapon disarms are rehearsed and analyzed in a variety of dangerous scenarios. Students also train with a large variety of equipment, including heavy bags, double-end bags, uppercut bags, pummel bags, focus mitts, striking shields, mirrors, rattan sticks, foam and plastic bats, kicking pads, knife drones, trigger-sensitive (mock) guns, boxing and digit gloves, full-body armor, and hundreds of different environmental props.

There are more than two hundred unique training methodologies used in Contemporary Fighting Arts. Each one is scientifically designed to prepare students for the hard-core realities of real world combat. There are also three specific training methodologies used to develop and sharpen the fundamental attributes and skills of armed and unarmed fighting, including proficiency training, conditioning training, and street training.

Proficiency training can be used for both armed and unarmed skills. When conducted properly, proficiency training develops speed, power, accuracy, non-telegraphic movement, balance, and general psychomotor skill. The training objective is to sharpen one specific body weapon, maneuver, or technique at a time by executing it over and over for a prescribed number of repetitions. Each time the technique or maneuver is executed with "clean" form at various speeds. Movements are also performed with the eyes closed to develop a kinesthetic "feel" for the action. Proficiency training can be accomplished through the use of various types of equipment, including the heavy bag, double-end bag, focus mitts, training knives, real and mock pistols, striking shields, shin and knee guards, foam and plastic bats, mannequin heads, and so on.

Conditioning training develops endurance, fluidity, rhythm, distancing, timing, speed, footwork, and balance. In most cases, this type of training requires the student to deliver a variety of fighting combinations for three- or four-minute rounds separated by 30-second breaks. Like proficiency training, this type of training can also be performed at various speeds. A good workout consists of at least five rounds. Conditioning training can be performed on the bags with full-contact sparring gear, rubber training knives, focus mitts, kicking shields, and shin guards, or against imaginary assailants in shadow fighting.

Conditioning training is not necessarily limited to just three-

or four-minute rounds. For example, CFA's ground fighting training can last as long as 30 minutes. The bottom line is that it all depends on what you are training for.

Street training is the final preparation for the real thing. Since many violent altercations are explosive, lasting an average of 20 seconds, you must prepare for this possible scenario. This means delivering explosive and powerful compound attacks with vicious intent for approximately 20 seconds, resting one minute, and then repeating the process.

Street training prepares you for the stress and immediate fatigue of a real fight. It also develops speed, power, explosiveness, target selection and recognition, timing, footwork, pacing, and breath control. You should practice this methodology in different lighting, on different terrains, and in different environmental settings. You can use different types of training equipment as well. For example, you can prepare yourself for multiple assailants by having your training partners attack you with focus mitts from a variety of angles, ranges, and target postures. For 20 seconds, go after them with vicious low-line kicks, powerful punches, and devastating strikes.

When all is said and done, the physical component creates a fighter who is physically fit and armed with a lethal arsenal of tools, techniques, and weapons that can be deployed with destructive results.

The Mental Component

The mental component of CFA focuses on the cerebral aspects of a fighter, developing killer instinct, strategic/tactical awareness, analysis and integration skills, philosophy, and cognitive skills.

The Killer Instinct

Deep within each of us is a cold and deadly primal power known as the "killer instinct." The killer instinct is a vicious combat mentality that surges to your consciousness and turns you into a fierce fighter who is free of fear, anger, and apprehension. If you want to survive the horrifying dynamics of real criminal violence, you must cultivate and utilize this instinctive killer mentality.

There are 14 characteristics of CFA's killer instinct. They are: (1) clear and lucid thinking, (2) heightened situational awareness, (3) adrenaline surge, (4) mobilized body, (5) psychomotor control, (6) absence of distraction, (7) tunnel vision, (8) fearless mind-set, (9) tactical implementation, (10) the lack of emotion, (11) breath control, (12) pseudospeciation, (13) viciousness, and (14) pain tolerance.

Visualization and crisis rehearsal are just two techniques

14

used to develop, refine, and channel this extraordinary source of strength and energy so that it can be used to its full potential.

Strategic/Tactical Awareness

Strategy is the bedrock of preparedness. In CFA, there are three unique categories of strategic awareness that will diminish the likelihood of criminal victimization. They are criminal awareness, situational awareness, and self-awareness. When developed, these essential skills prepare you to assess a wide variety of threats instantaneously and accurately. Once you've made a proper threat assessment, you will be able to choose one of the following five self-defense options: comply, escape, de-escalate, assert, or fight back.

CFA also teaches students to assess a variety of other important factors, including the assailant's demeanor, intent, range, positioning and weapon capability, as well as such environmental issues as escape routes, barriers, terrain, and makeshift weaponry. In addition to assessment skills, CFA also teaches students how to enhance perception and

15

observation skills.

Analysis and Integration Skills

The analytical process is intricately linked to understanding how to defend yourself in any threatening situation. If you want to be the best, every aspect of fighting and personal protection must be dissected. Every strategy, tactic, movement, and concept must be broken down to its atomic parts. The three planes (physical, mental, spiritual) of self-defense must be unified through arduous practice and constant exploration.

CFA's most advanced practitioners have sound insight and understanding of a wide range of sciences and disciplines. They include human anatomy, kinesiology, criminal justice, sociology, kinesics, proxemics, combat physics, emergency medicine, crisis management, histrionics, police and military science, the psychology of aggression, and the role of archetypes.

Analytical exercises are also a regular part of CFA training. For example, we conduct problem-solving sessions involving particular assailants attacking in defined environments. We move hypothetical attackers through various ranges to provide insight into tactical solutions. We scrutinize different methods of attack for their general utility in combat. We also discuss the legal ramifications of self-defense on a frequent basis.

In addition to problem-solving sessions, students are slowly exposed to concepts of integration and modification. Oral and written examinations are given to measure intellectual accomplishment. Unlike systems, CFA does not use colored belts or sashes to identify the student's level of proficiency.

Philosophy

Philosophical resolution is essential to a fighter's mental confidence and clarity. Anyone learning the art of war must find the ultimate answers to questions concerning the use of violence in defense of himself or others. To advance to the highest levels of combat awareness, you must find clear and lucid answers to such provocative questions as could you take the life of another, what are your fears, who are you, why are you interested in studying Contemporary Fighting Arts, why are you reading this book, and what is good and what is evil? If you haven't begun the quest to formulate these important questions and answers, then take a break. It's time to figure out just why you want to know the laws and rules of destruction.

Cognitive Combat Skills

Cognitive combat exercises are also important for improving one's fighting skills. CFA uses visualization and crisis rehearsal scenarios to improve general body mechanics, tools and techniques, and maneuvers, as well as tactic selection. Mental clarity, concentration, and emotional control are also developed to enhance one's ability to call upon the controlled killer instinct.

The Spiritual Component

There are many tough fighters out there. In fact, they reside in every town in every country. However, most are nothing more than vicious animals that lack self-mastery. And self-mastery is what separates the true warrior from the eternal novice.

I am not referring to religious precepts or beliefs when I

speak of CFA's spiritual component. Unlike most martial arts, CFA does not merge religion into its spiritual aspect. Religion is a very personal and private matter and should never, be incorporated into any fighting system. CFA's spiritual component is not something that is taught or studied. Rather, it is that which transcends the physical and mental aspects of being and reality. There is a deeper part of each of us that is a tremendous source of truth and accomplishment.

In CFA, the spiritual component is something that is slowly and progressively acquired. During the challenging quest of combat training, one begins to tap the higher qualities of human nature. Those elements of our being that inherently enable us to know right from wrong and good from evil. As we slowly develop this aspect of our total self, we begin to strengthen qualities profoundly important to the "truth." Such qualities are essential to your growth through the mastery of inner peace, the clarity of your "vision," and your recognition of universal truths.

One of the goals of my system is to promote virtue and moral responsibility in people who have extreme capacities for physical and mental destructiveness. The spiritual component of fighting is truly the most difficult aspect of personal growth. Yet, unlike the physical component, where the practitioner's abilities will be limited to some degree by genetics and other natural factors, the spiritual component of combat offers unlimited potential for growth and development. In the final analysis, CFA's spiritual component poses the greatest challenges for the student. It is an open-ended plane of unlimited advancement.

CHAPTER ONE
Pressure Point Fighting

Making Sense of it All!

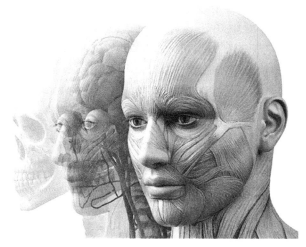

Pressure Point Fighting is a subject shrouded in mystery, intrigue, and tons of bullshit. Therefore, assigning a clear cut definition to the term "pressure point fighting" isn't such an easy task, because it has different meanings to different people, especially martial artists who possess a skewed perspective of reality.

Depending on the martial arts style or background, pressure point fighting can range from being functional and pragmatic, to downright idiotic.

In my reality based self-defense system, Contemporary Fighting Arts, our pressure point techniques differ drastically from other martial arts styles by focusing exclusively on real world self-defense applications.

My pressure point fighting methodology is efficient, effective and safe, which means you'll stand the best chances of survival when faced with a dangerous self-defense encounter. What more can anyone ask for?

Pressure Point Myths

I'm sure at some point you've heard stories about mysterious kung-fu masters who can effortlessly destroy a larger and stronger foe with a simple touch of their magical hand. Or perhaps, you've heard about the Zen master who can kill you with just the slightest touch of his index finger – also known as the death touch or "dim mak."

For those of you who believe such nonsense, I've got some fantastic beachfront property in Kansas that I want to sell to you. Trust me, bro, it's dirt cheap!

Now, for those people who aren't familiar with me and my background, I'm a martial arts innovator with over 35 years of teaching and training reality based self-defense, and I can assure you that such pressure point stories are nothing more than fairy tales, absolute nonsense that deserves the very same credibility as Krampus or Slender Man.

Sadly enough, there's droves of gullible people who believe such crap, and actually devote a good portion of their lives to

its study and practice. P.T. Barnum was right when he said, "There's a sucker born every minute." And there's no shortage of them in the martial arts world.

Don't get me wrong, it is possible to neutralize a formidable adversary with one strategically placed blow, but it has absolutely nothing to do with mystical Chi energy, ancient Zen masters, or esoteric teachings. Remember, if something is too good to be true, it often is.

I do anticipate some backlash for the things I will say in this book. And for those myopic few who find my opinions insensitive or disrespectful, I strongly suggest putting this book down and reading something else. Perhaps "100 Magic Tricks" or "Cosplay for Dummies."

Fortunately, I don't care what fools think of my work. Never have, never will. Besides, I've always had a very specific target audience… practical people who want real-world self-defense solutions, devoid of "hopium" and bullshit. For those people, please read on.

There will always be gullible people willing to believe in myths.

23

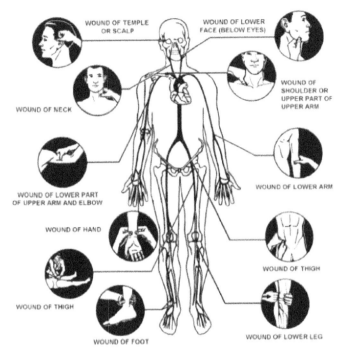

Pictured above, classic examples of pressure point target myths. Sorry folks, this crap will get you killed in a real fight.

Combat Pressure Points

So what are combat pressure points? And how do they relate to real-world fighting? In one of my previous books, I gave a very basic definition of pressure points. I wrote, "A pressure point is a vulnerable anatomical target where a nerve lies close to its surface and is supported by bone or muscle mass."

However, there's much more to combat pressure points than meets the eyes. In fact, they're not just vulnerable to strikes. They can also be compressed, resulting in serious damage for the adversary.

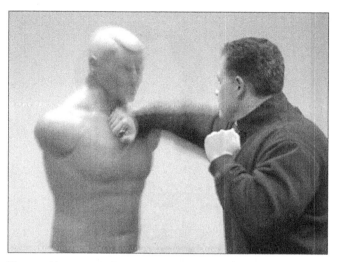

Pictured here, a kubotan striking a pressure point target.

For example, the throat region is a "compression pressure point" that can be exploited with a rear naked choke technique, requiring you to simultaneously compress both the carotid artery and vegus nerve with your forearms.

Moreover, a strong and prolonged compression to a pressure point target may cause some of the following physiological responses to occur:

- **Motor dysfunction**
- **Balance disruption**
- **Extreme pain**
- **Involuntary muscular spasms**
- **Drooling**
- **Disorientation**
- **Loss of consciousness**
- **Loss of bodily functions**
- **Possible death**

The rear naked choke is one of the most effective compression point techniques known to man.

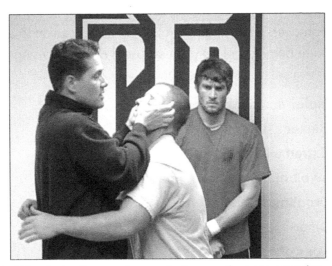

In this photo, Franco demonstrates another compression pressure point technique called the Double Thumb Gouge.

Two Pressure Point Categories

Now that we have an understanding that pressure points can be either struck or compressed, it's time to look into the two possible categories, each with separate objectives. They include:

- **Pain Compliance Pressure Points** - used to gain immediate compliance from the adversary through the application of specific locks and holds. This is particularly useful for security personnel, law enforcement, and various types of low-level conflicts.

- **Incapacitation Pressure Points** - includes both blood flow restriction and impact techniques that immediately incapacitate the adversary. These knock-out pressure points can also range from intermediate to deadly force applications.

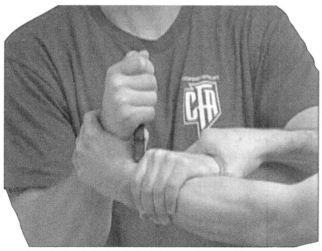

Here, the student demonstrates a pain compliance pressure point with a kubotan.

Incapacitation Pressure Points

For the purposes of this book, I'm going to focus exclusively on *Incapacitation Pressure Points* that can be readily applied under the stress of real-world combat conditions.

The term "incapacitation pressure points" means different things to different people. For example, according to some practitioners, incapacitation pressure points are targets which cause brief dizziness for the adversary; a dizziness that causes the opponent's knees to weaken or buckle.

Sadly, such a definition is inaccurate and certainly impractical for real world self-defense applications. Pressure point fighting techniques that simply promote "transitory dizziness" are inadequate for real-world self-defense conditions. Never forget this.

In most cases, transitory dizziness won't work on psychotics, drunks or drugged assailants as well as many other real world scenarios. For example, consider the dangers of applying one of those "dizzying techniques" on an enraged attacker high on PCP. Frankly, you'll have a snowball's chance in hell of surviving the encounter.

In real world self-defense, time is a critical factor! You must employ practical street fighting techniques that produce instant results. Therefore, the only safe and sure-fire method of pressure point fighting are those techniques that produce immediate results... 100% Incapacitation!

And since we're only concerned with real world self-defense applications, I define incapacitation pressure points as anatomical targets which cause a complete and immediate loss of consciousness or impairment for the adversary.

As I said earlier, there's only two effective ways to apply incapacitation pressure points that causes a complete and immediate loss of consciousness for the adversary, impact and blood flow pressure points. Let's take a quick look at each one.

Impact Pressure Points – these are vital and sensitive anatomical targets that can be struck with your limbs. For example, knocking someone out with a power punch. Impact knockout pressure points can also be struck with various hand held weapons, such as the kubotan, mini flashlight, combat stick, or club.

Blood Flow Pressure Points – when deliberate pressure is applied to these life sustaining targets, immediate unconsciousness and possible death can occur.

Now that you have a fundamental understanding of Incapacitation Pressure Points, it's time to take a look at some of the tactical advantages of pressure point fighting.

Pressure Point Advantages

Let's take a look at several compelling reasons why you should consider adding pressure point fighting to your self-defense arsenal:

Maximize Your Odds of Winning

Every self-defense situation needs to be won fast. Period! Remember, the longer a fight lasts, the greater your chances of serious injury or even death. Every technique and tactic that you apply in a fight must be efficient, effective and provide the least amount of danger and risk.

Pressure point fighting is one of the best methods of achieving these three objectives because it allows you to incapacitate your assailant swiftly while, at the same time, negating his ability to retaliate. As a result, no time is wasted, and no unnecessary risks are taken.

It's Difficult to Recover From It

There's an old saying, "The hardest punch, is the one you never see coming." Truer words have never been spoken, especially when it comes to the art and science of pressure point fighting.

The element of surprise is invaluable in a fight, and pressure points instantly gives you a substantial advantage over your adversary by allowing you to quickly overwhelm his mind and body. In other words, you demolish his defenses and take him out of the fight.

It's a Great Equalizer

Knock-out pressure points are great equalizers, especially when they're delivered non-telegraphically with your hands. In fact, a properly placed pressure point hit can defeat anyone, regardless of their size or strength. This is especially important when you're confronted with a larger and stronger adversary who's hell-bent on putting you in the hospital.

Moreover, nothing can be more dangerous than defending against multiple attackers. Fortunately, pressure point fighting is an essential street survival technique when faced with such a perilous situation.

In both my instructional video and book titled The 10 Best Ways to Defeat Multiple Attackers, I discuss the vital importance of delivering a preemptive strike to the leader or "alpha" of the pack first. In most cases, he's the one who controls the spirit of the group and motivates the others to attack.

A strategically placed pressure point strike can make all the difference during a multiple attacker assault.

Because of the extreme threat and danger posed by multiple assailants, it's essential to make an example of the leader by severely injuring or crippling him. For example, if the others accomplices see their buddy violently choking from a pressure point strike to the throat, they'll be less inclined to continue their assault on you.

Nature of The Beast

In order to prevent being victimized by a pressure point strike, you must know how to apply it yourself. In essence, you must understand the *nature of the beast*. You've got to open your ears, eyes, and mind to the many techniques, tactics, strategies of a skilled fighter. This will greatly enhance your ability to avoid such attacks and, beyond that, to deal with a particular attack if it occurs.

He who hits first, often wins!

In most fights, if you don't initiate the first strike, your adversary most likely will. Allowing the opponent the opportunity to deliver the first punch is extremely dangerous. It's like allowing a gunslinger to draw his weapon first. If he's a good shot, you are done!

In pressure point fighting, if you allow the assailant to strike you first, he might injure or possibly kill you, and he will most certainly force you into an irreversible series of defensive moves that will inhibit you from issuing an effective counterattack.

The First Strike Connection

Therefore, whenever you are threatened by a dangerous adversary and there is no way to escape safely, you must strike first, strike fast, strike with authority, and keep the pressure on. This offensive strategy is known as the **first strike principle**, and it's essential to the process of neutralizing a formidable adversary in a self-defense altercation.

Basically, a first strike is defined as the strategic application of proactive force designed to interrupt the initial stages of an assault before it becomes a self-defense crisis.

One inescapable fact about street self-defense is that the longer the fight lasts, the greater your chances of serious injury or even death. Common sense suggests that you must end the fight as quickly as possible. Striking first is the best method of achieving this tactical objective because it permits you to neutralize your assailant swiftly while, at the same time, precluding his ability to retaliate effectively. No time is wasted, and no unnecessary risks are taken.

When it comes to reality based self-defense, the element of surprise is invaluable. Launching the first strike gives you the upper hand because it allows you to hit the criminal adversary suddenly and unexpectedly. As a result, you demolish his defenses and ultimately take him out of the fight.

CHAPTER TWO
Targets

Pressure Point Fighting Targets

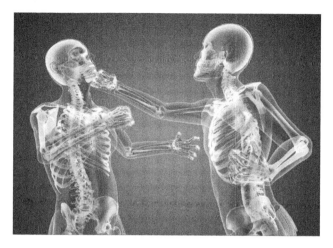

I could write several books addressing different pressure point targets as they relate to self-defense and personal protection, but for the purposes of our needs, I will focus on *incapacitation pressure point targets*.

This requires us to focus on the assailant's head, or what I call *"head hunting."* Consequently, the pressure point targets covered in this chapter will include the following anatomical targets:

- **Eyes**
- **Ears**
- **Temple**
- **Nose**
- **Chin**
- **Back of Neck**
- **Throat**

The Eyes

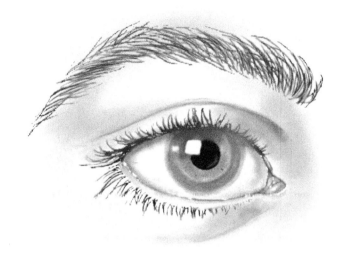

The eyes are ideal pressure point targets because they are extremely sensitive and difficult to protect from an attack. Best of all, striking them requires very little force.

The eyes can be poked, scratched, and gouged from a variety of angles. Depending on the force of your strike, it can cause numerous injuries, including watering of the eyes, hemorrhaging, blurred vision, temporary or permanent blindness, severe pain, rupture, shock, and unconsciousness.

The probable reaction dynamic from a well targeted eye strike may include the following:

- The opponent bends forward, shuts his eyes.
- The opponent covers his eyes with his hands.
- The opponent freezes from shock.

Finger Jab Drill

The finger jab is the mother of all eye strikes. This technique is a quick, non-telegraphic strike executed from your lead arm. Contact is made with your fingertips, and it's likened to speed of a snakebite.

To execute the finger jab properly, quickly shoot your arm out and back. Don't tense your muscles prior to the execution of the strike. Just relax and send it out. Targets for the finger-jab are the assailant's eyes.

Don't forget that a finger jab strike can cause temporary or permanent blindness, severe pain, and shock. With the finger jab, you want speed, accuracy, and, above all, non-telegraphic movement.

X-Ray Chart Drill

Another effective way for developing the retraction speed of a finger jab strike is to practice on an x-ray chart. Always remember to focus on delivering lightning fast strikes.

Step 1.

Step 2.

Thumb Rake Drill

The thumb rake is another effective eye attack technique used in close-quarter combat. Here, the practitioner acquires the inside position and uses his thumb to rake across the eye. Notice how his other hand anchors the neck for stability and control. Perform this drill using both right and left hands.

Thumb Gouge Variation

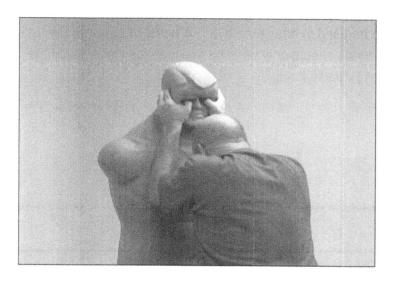

The double-thumb gouge is a compression pressure point that produces devastating results. This tactic can be delivered when either standing or fighting on the ground.

To perform the gouge, place both hands on the assailant's face. Stabilize your hands by wrapping your bottom fingers around both sides of your assailant's jaw. Immediately drive both your right and left thumbs into the assailant's eye sockets. Maintain and increase forceful pressure. The double-thumb gouge can cause temporary or permanent blindness, shock and unconsciousness.

WARNING: *The double thumb gouge should only be used in life and death situations! Be certain that it is legally warranted and justified.*

Weapon Strikes

The kubotan, tactical cane, and other hand-held weapons can be used to attack the eyes. *A word of caution,* hand-held weapons should only be used in situations that warrant the use of deadly force.

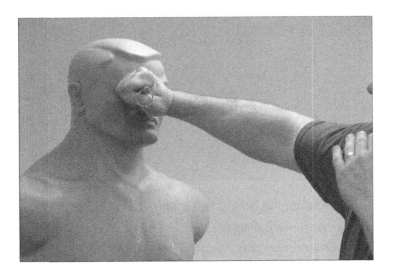

The Ears

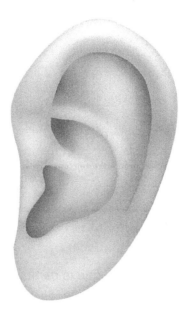

Like the eyes, the ears are extremely sensitive to attack. The opponent's ears can be punched, popped, and torn. When struck with a moderate amount of force, the tympanic membrane (eardrum) will easily rupture. Striking the ear can also result in percussive shock, extreme pain, unconsciousness, partial or complete loss of hearing, bleeding, disorientation and loss of balance.

Two-Hand Ear Pop

This pressure point technique is particularly effective when a larger and stronger adversary places you in a front bear hug, leaving both of your hands to counter attack. I can tell you from firsthand experience, this technique is extremely effective and will force your adversary to release his hold immediately.

Step 1.

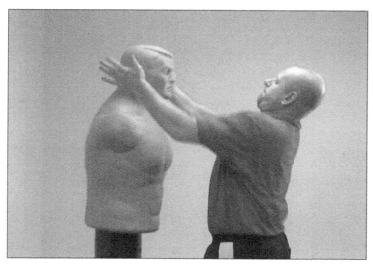

Step 2: Notice how the practitioner arches his back to simulate a powerful front bear hug.

Hooks to Ears

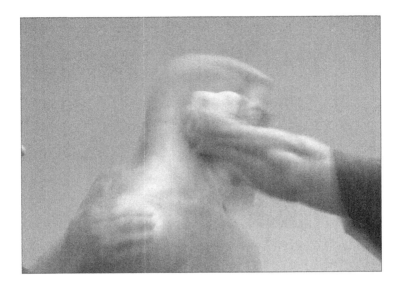

Hook punches are considered to be the heavy artillery. Here, a student demonstrates a lead and rear hook punch directed to the opponent's ears.

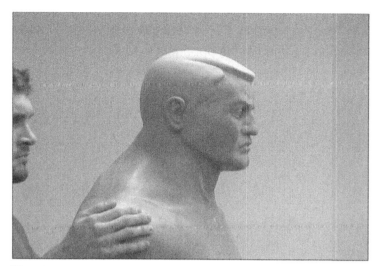

Step 1.

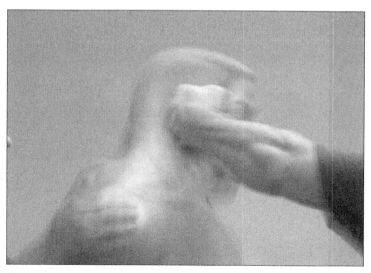

Step 2.

49

Elbows to Ears

Like the hook punch, the elbows can also yield devastating result when targeted at the opponent's ears.

Knees to Ears

Ear strikes are not just limited to stand-up combat. You can also strike with your knees when ground fighting.

Here, the practitioner drives knee strikes into the ear from the side mount position. **A word of caution**: Delivering knee strikes to the head region can be deadly and should on be used in situations that warrant the application of deadly force.

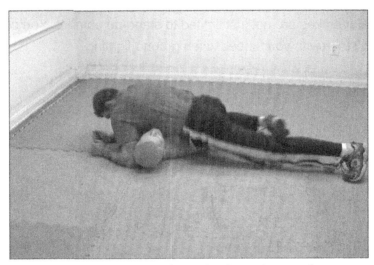

Step 1: After sabilizing your base, load your knee strike.

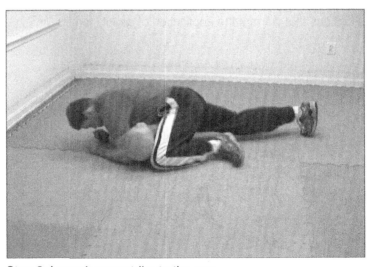

Step 2: Launch your strike to the ear.

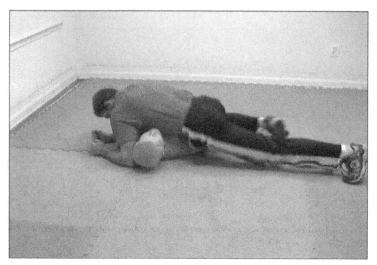

Step 3: Reload your knee strike.

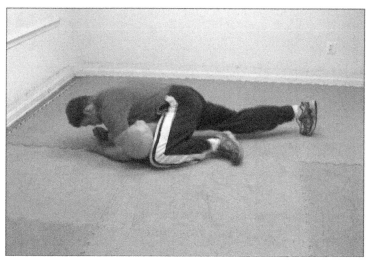

Step 4: Strike again.

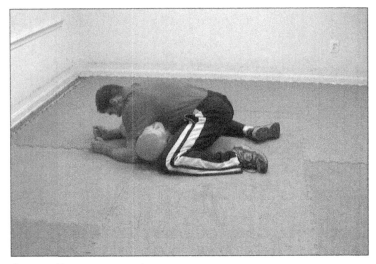

Step 5: Return to your base.

The Temple

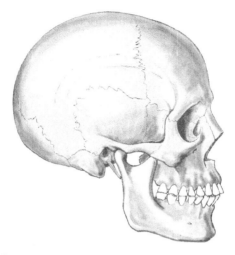

The temple or sphenoid bone is a thin, weak bone located on the side of the skull approximately one-inch from the eyes. Because of its fragile structure and close proximity to the brain, a powerful strike to this pressure point target can be deadly. Other possible injuries include unconsciousness, hemorrhage, concussion, shock, and coma.

Focus Mitt Hooks (to Temple)

If you can't get your hands on a heavy bag, you can also use the focus mitts to develop the technique.

Step 1.

Step 2.

Body Opponent Bag Hooks

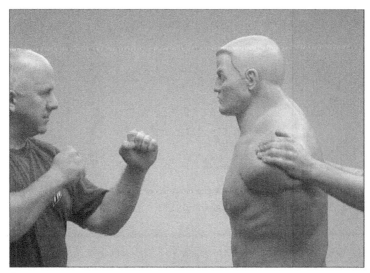

Step 1.

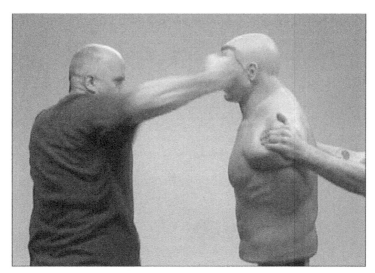

Step 2.

Stick Strikes to Temple

Attacking the temple is not just limited to natural body weapons. In fact, you can use hand-held weapons like the kubotan, tactical cane, and the stick on the body opponent bag.

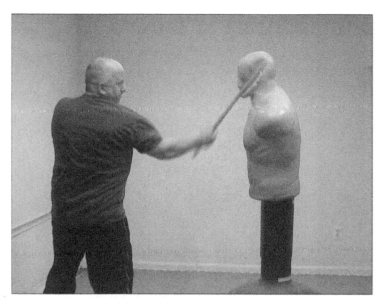

Here, the practitioner practices basic strikes to the temple region on the body opponent bag. Keep in mind that effective stick fighting skills require significant time to master. Be patient and it will come.

Kubotan Strike to Temple

A Kubotan strike to the temple can produce devastating result, and should only be used in life and death situations that legally warrant the use of deadly force.

Tactical pens and flashlights can also be used to strike the temple with devastating results. Again, be certain your actions are legally justified in the eyes of the law!

The Nose

The nose is made up of a thin bone, cartilage, numerous blood vessels, and many nerves. It is a particularly good target because it stands out from the criminal's face and can be struck from three different directions (upwards, straight, downwards).

A moderate blow can cause stunning pain, eye-watering, temporary blindness, and hemorrhaging. A powerful strike can result in shock and unconsciousness.

Short Arc Hammer Fist to Nose (Body Opponent Bag)

The Short Arc Hammer Fist is a fantastic close-quarter strike that can easily shatter the assailant's nose. This legendary "first strike" technique is incredibly deceptive, and virtually impossible to stop.

To deliver the hammer fist, begin by raising your fist with your elbow flexed. Quickly whip your clenched fist down in a vertical line onto the bridge of your assailant's nose. Remember to keep your elbow bent on impact and maintain your balance throughout execution.

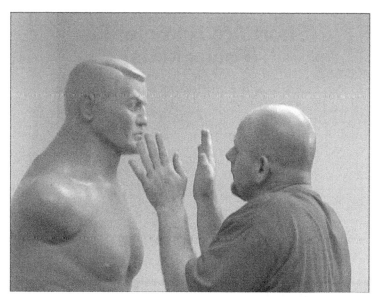

Step 1.

Step 2.

65

Short Arc Hammer Fist
(Focus Mitts)

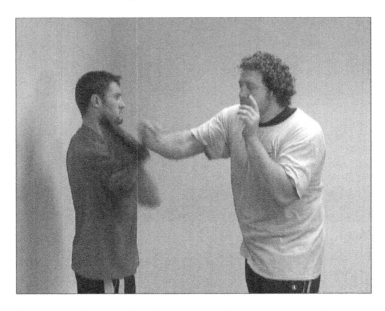

If you don't own a body opponent bag, you can always use the focus mitt to develop the short arc technique. Be certain you training partner holds the focus mitt at the proper hight and angle.

Step 1.

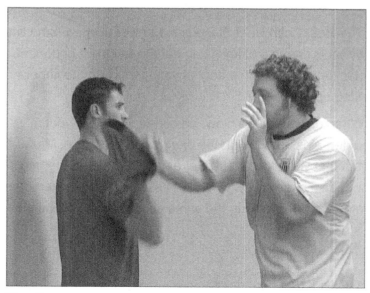

Step 2.

Rear Palm Heel to Nose
(Body Opponent Bag)

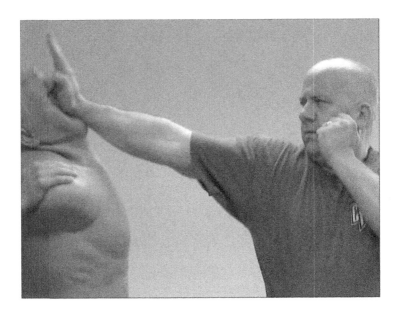

The Rear Palm Heel Strike is s a powerful open-hand linear blow that is capable of knocking out the toughest opponent. Contact is made with the heel of your palm with the fingers pointing up.

When delivering the blow, be certain to torque your shoulder, hips, and foot in the direction of the strike. Make certain that your arm extends straight out and that the heel of your palm makes contact with the assailant's nose. Remember to retract your arm along the same line in which you initiated the strike.

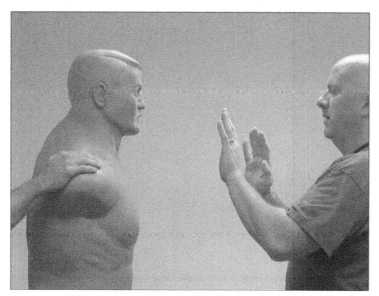

Step 1.

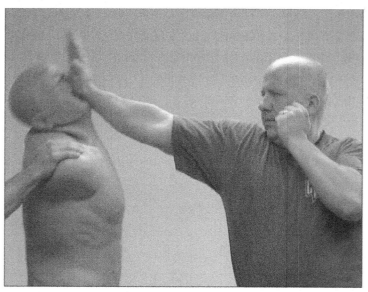

Step 2.

Rear Palm Heel to Nose
(Focus Mitts)

Again, if you don't own a body opponent bag, you can still develop the rear palm heel with the ficus mitts. Just be certain your training partner holds the mitts at the correct angle and height, accurately representing a nose target.

Step 1.

Step 2.

71

Septum Pull Technique

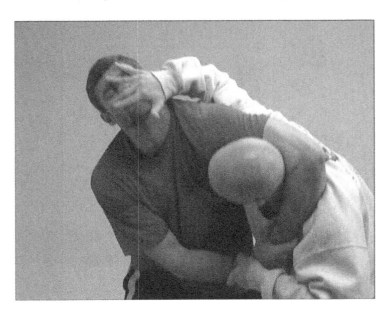

The Septum Pull is a compression pressure point technique used to counter a side head lock. The septum is especially sensitive and it's located directly under the assailant's nose.

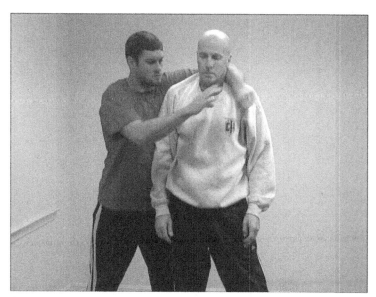

Step 1: The assailant attacks with a side head lock.

Step 2: Avoid the urge to fight against the lock. Instead, turn your head into the attacker's centerline.

Step 3: Trap the attacker's striking hand with your left hand.

Step 4: Reach over the attacker's head, placing your middle finger firmly under the assailant's nose (septum region).

74

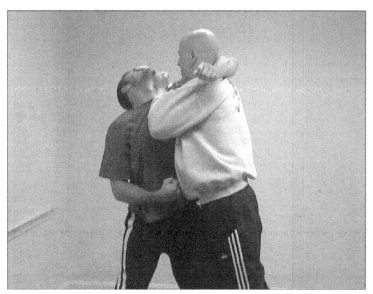

Step 5: Force the attacker's head back, and immediately
counter with a hammer fist blow to his throat.

Uppercut to Nose
(Focus Mitts)

Frequently, your adversary will double over during the course of a fight, allowing you to exploit the situation by delivering an uppercut strike to his nose.

To execute the rear uppercut, quickly twist and lift the rear side of your body into the direction of the blow. Make certain that the blow has a tight arc and that you avoid any telegraphing.

Finally, notice how the focus mitt is held at a level that represents a nose target, as opposed to a chin target.

Step 1.

Step 2.

Vertical Knee to to Nose
(Focus Mitts)

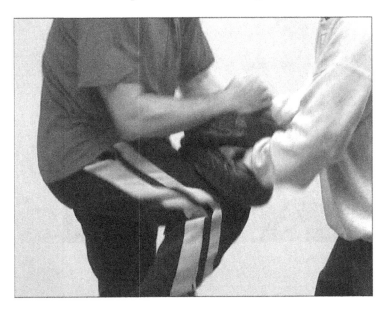

Another method of exploiting an adversary who doubles over during a fight is to attack him with vertical knee strikes to the nose. In the following photo sequence, the practitioner (left) is pushed through an endurance knee strike drill performed on the focus mitts.

Step 1.

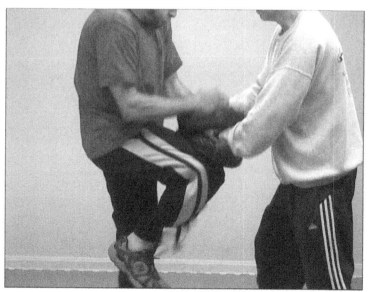

Step 2.

The Chin

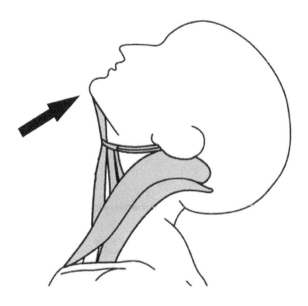

In western boxing, the chin is considered a "knockout button" responsible for retiring countless boxers. The chin is also a great pressure point target for unarmed combat.

When the chin is struck at a forty-five degree angle, shock waves are transmitted to the cerebellum and cerebral hemispheres of the brain, resulting in paralysis and immediate unconsciousness.

Depending on the force of your blow, other possible injuries include broken jaw, concussion, and whiplash to the assailant's neck. Some of the best body weapons to strike the chin are: uppercuts, elbow strikes, knee strikes, palm heels and even head butts.

Uppercut to Chin
(Body opponent Bag)

I can tell you, from first hand experience, that a strategically placed uppercut to the assailant chin will knock him out instantly. However, be careful! There have been several instances where a person was knocked out by an uppercut, causing him to lose consciousness, hitting his head on the pavement, and dying. Again, always be certain you self-defense actions are justified in the eyes of the law!

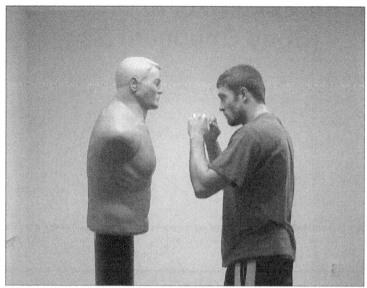

Step 1.

Step 2.

83

Palm Heel to Chin
(Body Opponent Bag)

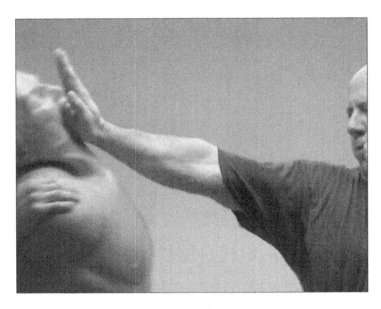

Palm Heel strikes are not just limited to the nose. You can also develop chin strikes on the body opponent bag.

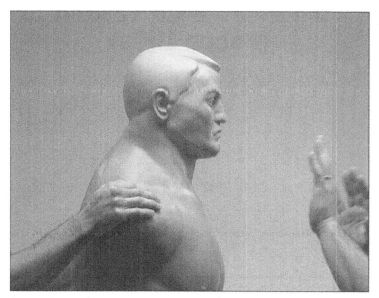

Step 1.

Step 2.

Vertical Elbow to Chin
(Focus Mitts)

The rear vertical elbow strike is ideal for attacking the chin at close-quarter combat range. Once again, you can use the focus mitts to sharpen the technique.

Step 1.

Step 2.

Uppercut to Chin
(Double End Bag)

When it comes to attacking pressure point targets, accuracy matters. A lot! The double end bag is a unique piece of equipment that will help you develop pin-point accuracy with your chin strikes.

Step 1.

Step 2.

89

Head Butt to Chin

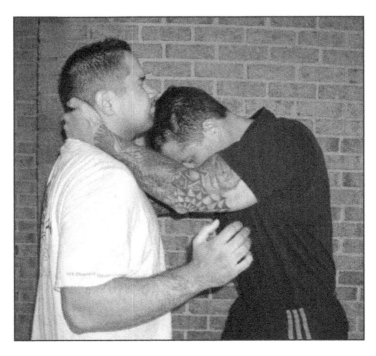

When fighting in close quarters, your head can be used for butting your assailant's chin. Head butts are also ideal when a strong attacker has placed you in a hold where your arms are pinned against your sides. Keep in mind that the head butt can be delivered in four different directions: forward, backward, right side, and left side.

Back of Neck

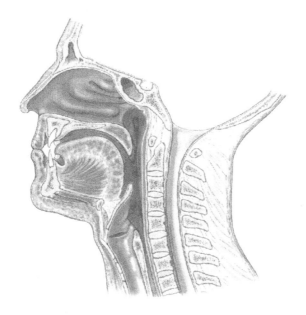

The back of the neck consists of the first seven vertebrae of the spinal column. They act as a circuit board for nerve impulses from the brain to the body.

The back of the neck is a lethal pressure point target because the vertebrae are poorly protected. A very powerful strike to the back of the neck can cause shock, unconsciousness, a broken neck, complete paralysis, coma, and death.

Long Arc Hammer Fist to Neck (Focus Mitts)

The Long Arc Hammer Fist strike to the back of the neck is a *finishing off technique* that should only be used in deadly force situations.

In the following photos, notice how the focus mitts are positioned at the proper height for the striker. Also, notice how the striker bends his knees and drops his weight when delivering the blow.

Step 1.

Step 2.

Stick Strike to Neck
(Focus Mitts)

The butt of a stick can be used to attack the back of the neck. Again, striking this pressure point target can be deadly, and should only be used in life and death self-defense situations.

Step 1.

Step 2.

Kubotan to Neck
(Focus Mitts)

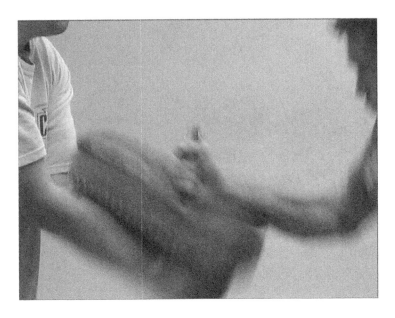

The kubotan is another hand-held weapon that can be used to strike the back of the assailants neck. Warning! Only use this technique in situations that warrant the use of deadly force.

Step 1.

Step 2.

Throat

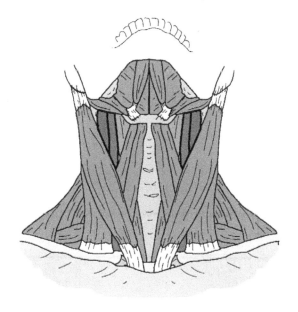

The throat is another lethal pressure point target because it is only protected by a thin layer of skin. This region consists of the thyroid, hyaline and crocoid cartilage, trachea, and larynx. The trachea, or windpipe, is a cartilaginous tube that measures 4 1/2 inches in length and is approximately 1 inch in diameter.

A powerful strike to this target can result in unconsciousness, blood drowning, massive hemorrhaging, air starvation, and death. If the thyroid cartilage is crushed, hemorrhaging will occur, the windpipe will quickly swell shut, resulting in suffocation.

Web Hand Strike to Throat
(Body Opponent Bag)

The Web Hand strike was originally featured in my book, *First Strike*, and it can be applied in both punching and grappling ranges of unarmed combat.

To perform the strike, simultaneously separate your thumb from your index finger and quickly drive the web of your hand into the adversary's throat. Be certain to keep your hand stiff with your palm down. Once contact is made, quickly retract your hand to the starting position.

WARNING: The web hand strike should only be used in life-and-death situations! Be certain that it is legally warranted and justified.

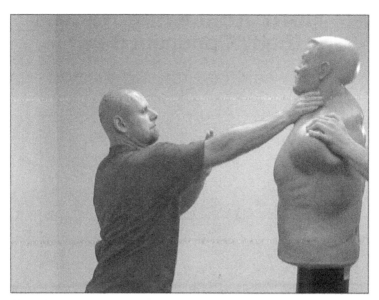

Step 1.

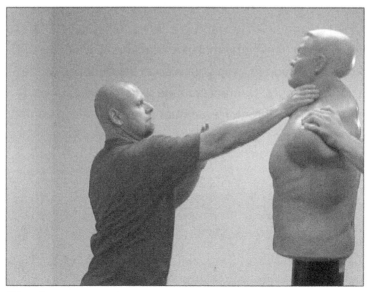

Step 2.

Horizontal Knife Hand
(Body Opponent Bag)

The Horizontal Knife Hand is a devastating strike that can be used when flanked by multiple attackers. Delivering the strike requires you to whip your hips in the direction of the flanking adversary. Contact is made with the edge of your hand against the throat. Remember to avoid making contact with your fingers.

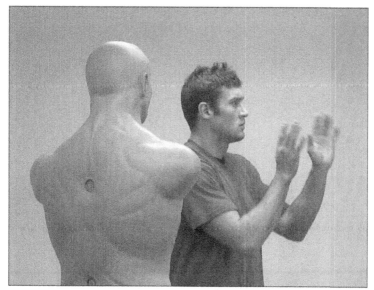

Step 1.

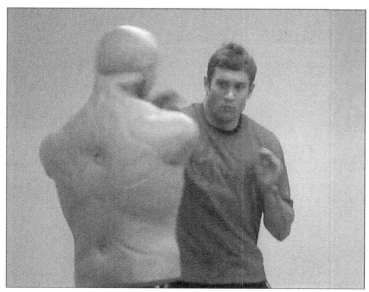

Step 2.

Multiple Opponent Scenarios

Step 1.

Step 2.

Step 3.

Throat Crush
(Septum Pull Variation)

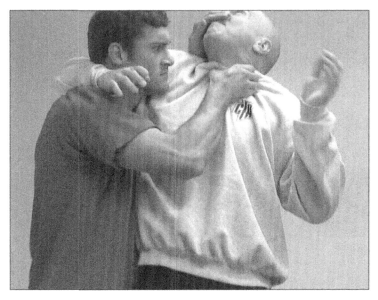

Earlier, I showed you how to escape a side head lock using a septum pull technique. Here is the very same move, except the practitioner finishes off his attacker with a throat crush technique. Again, this technique should only be used in life and death situations.

Step 1.

Step 2.

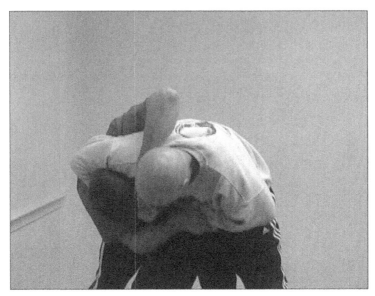

Step 3.

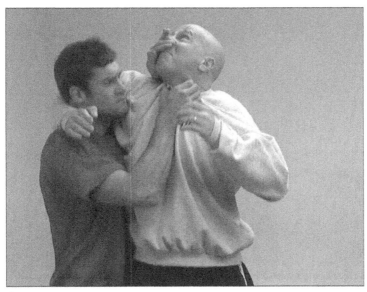

Step 4.

Forearm Choke
(From Mounted Position)

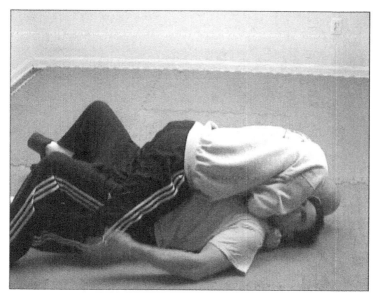

Attacking the throat is not just limited to stand up combat. You can also apply the forearm choke when ground fighting with your adversary.

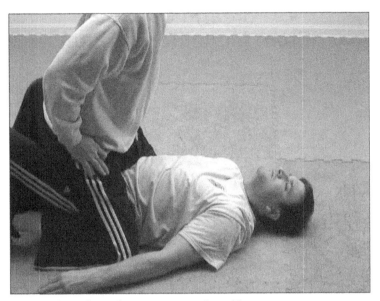

Step 1: Start from the top mounted position.

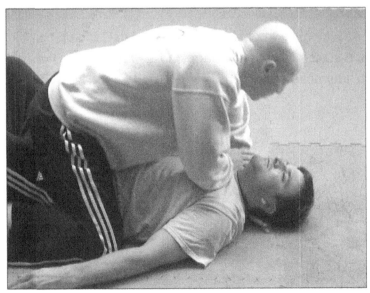

Step 2: Lower your base, slide your left forearm under the opponent's neck while simultaneously placing your right forearm across his throat.

110

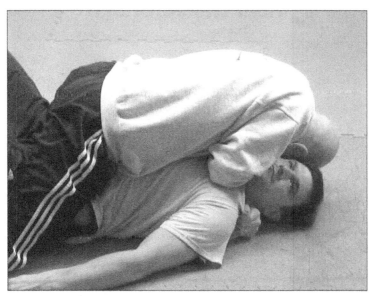

Step 3: Grab his shirt with your left hand, and grapevine your legs through his.

Step 4: Drop your weight down, tuck your head to the side, and scissor your forearms together.

Rear Naked Choke

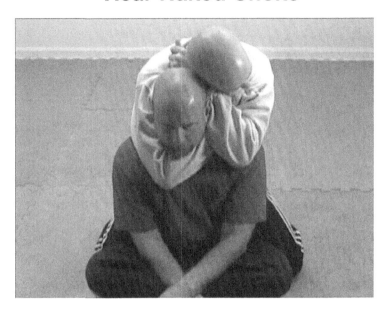

The Rear Naked Choke is one of the most effective submission techniques in your ground fighting arsenal. It can be applied from a standing, kneeling and prone position.

Ironically, you're not attacking the throat when performing this technique, but rather the carotid artery and the vegus nerve. Nevertheless, it's still classified as a throat region pressure point target.

Finally, don't forget that all types of choking techniques can be deadly, and should only be used when deadly force is warranted and justified in the eyes of the law!

Step 1.

Step 2.

113

Step 3.

Step 4.

CHAPTER THREE
The Backup Plan

Murphy's Law

Murphy's Law states "Anything that can go wrong will go wrong." And while the ultimate goal of pressure point fighting is to quickly put an end to a fight, you must have a backup plan in case you miss your target or your strike doesn't neutralize the threat. Remember, you cannot afford the risk that one perfectly executed pressure point technique will terminate the fight.

To drive the point home, think of the now familiar law enforcement stories of drug-induced criminal aggressors who keep coming after being hit by a .40 caliber bullet. There are a lot of those types of people out there, and they're often involved in violent street attacks.

The bottom line is, you cannot rely on a pressure point target to stop such a dangerous assailant. In almost every case you won't know your aggressor's pain tolerance, his state of mind or capability for violence.

However, there's nothing wrong with developing the capability to incapacitate your opponent out with a single blow. In fact, it can be done if you are willing to invest the time and energy to pressure point training.

Just remember, it might take more than just strike to stop your adversary. To complete the job, you might have to initiate a strategic compound attack.

Compound Your Strikes

A compound attack is what immediately follows your pressure point strike, and it's defined as the logical sequence of two or more tools strategically thrown in succession. The objective is to take the fight out of the assailant and the assailant out of the fight by destroying his defenses with a flurry of full-speed, full-force strikes.

Based on power, accuracy, speed and commitment, the compound attack also requires calculation, control and clarity. In other words, the unskilled, untrained brawler who goes off with a buzzsaw of violent strikes is not executing a compound attack. There is more to it than that.

The compound attack starts with a thorough understanding and knowledge of every conceivable anatomical target presented by the various stances, angles, distances, and movements of the opponent. Unless he is in full body armor, there are always targets. It is a question of recognizing them and striking quickly with the appropriate tools. This requires mastery of a wide range of offensive techniques, a complete understanding of combat ranges, reaction dynamic awareness, and the proper use of force.

But remember, what is universally true for all opponents is equally true for you. If there is always a target available on him, there's always one on you – although vulnerability can be reduced with proper training. Remember, strike first, strike fast, strike with authority, and keep the pressure on.

As you attack one target, others open up naturally. It is up to you to recognize them through reaction dynamic awareness and keep the offensive flow. Executed properly, the compound attack demolishes your opponents defenses that you ultimately take him down and out. It sounds great, but you must realize that it has to happen within seconds.

Therefore, in order to deliver a compound attack, you'll need to have a good understanding of secondary targets.

Compound Attack Example

Step 1.

Step 2.

Step 3.

Step 4.

Step 5.

Step 6.

Secondary Targets

Secondary targets are used in the event you're required to "follow-up" with a second or third offensive strike. For example, in the event your pressure point target fails to stop your adversary from committing further acts of aggression. This is what comprises the bulk of a compound attack. Follow-up targets can include the following:

- **Solar Plexus**

- **Ribs**

- **Groin**

- **Thighs**

- **Knees**

- **Shins**

- **Fingers**

- **Toes/Instep**

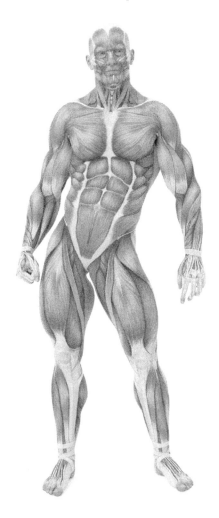

Solar Plexus

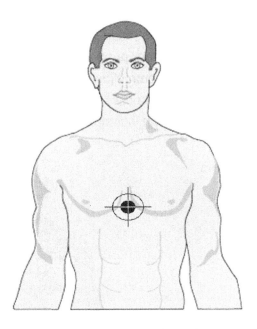

The solar plexus is a large collection of nerves situated below the sternum in the upper abdomen. A moderate blow to this area will cause nausea, tremendous pain, and shock, making it difficult for the assailant to breathe. A powerful strike to the solar plexus can result in severe abdominal pain and cramping, air starvation, and shock.

Step 1.

Step 2.

127

Ribs

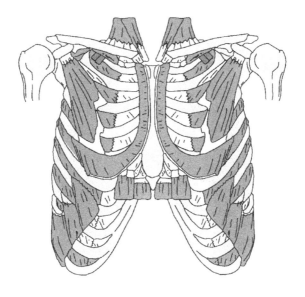

There are 12 pair of ribs in the human body. Excluding the eleventh and twelfth ribs, they are long and slender bones that are joined by the vertebral column in the back and the sternum and costal cartilage in the front.

Since there are no eleventh and twelfth ribs (floating ribs) in the front, you should direct your strikes to the ninth and tenth ribs. A moderate strike to the anterior region of the ribs will cause severe pain and shortness of breath. A powerful 45-degree blow could easily break a rib and force it into a lung, resulting in its collapse, internal hemorrhaging, severe pain, air starvation, unconsciousness, and possible death.

Step 1.

Step 2.

Groin

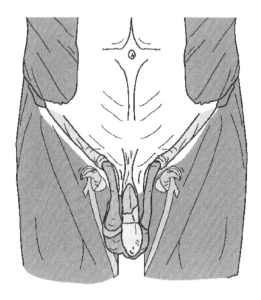

Everyone man will agree the genitals are highly sensitive organs. Even a light strike can be debilitating. A moderate strike to the groin can result in severe pain, nausea, vomiting, shortness of breath, and possible sterility. A powerful blow to the groin can crush the scrotum and testes against the pubic bones, causing shock and unconsciousness.

Step 1.

Step 2.

131

Thighs

Many people don't realize that the thighs are also vulnerable targets. A moderate kick to the rectus femoris or vastus lateralis muscles will result in immediate immobility of the leg. An extremely hard kick to the thigh can result in a fracture of the femur, resulting in internal bleeding, severe pain, cramping, and immobility of the broken leg.

Step 1.

Step 2.

133

Knees

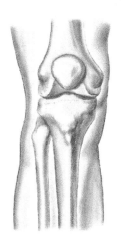 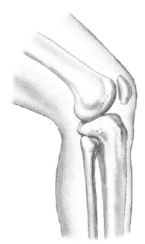

The knees are relatively weak joints that are held together by a number of supporting ligaments. When the assailant's leg is locked or fixed in position and a forceful strike is delivered to the front of the joint, the cruciate ligaments will tear, resulting in excruciating pain, swelling, and immobility. Located on the front of the knee joint is the patella, which is made of a small, loose piece of bone. The patella is also vulnerable to possible dislocation by a direct, forceful kick. Severe pain, swelling, and immobility may also result.

Pictured here, the author demonstrates a low-line side kick to his opponent's knee.

Shins

Like the thighs, the shins are excellent striking targets because they are very difficult to protect. The shins are also very sensitive because they are only protected by a thin layer of shin. A powerful kick delivered to this target may easily fracture it, resulting in extreme pain, hemorrhaging, and immobility of the afflicted leg.

Pictured here, a low-line side kick to the shin.

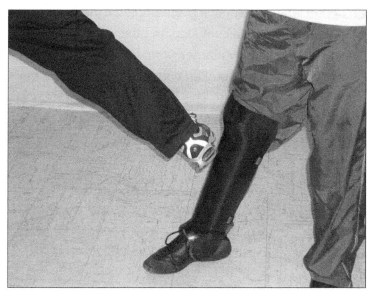

Target accuracy can be developed using shin guards.

Fingers

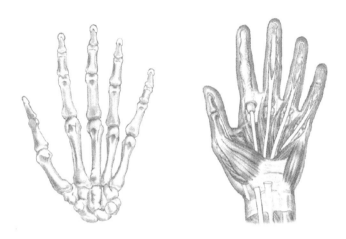

There's little question that the fingers can easily be broken when appreciable leverage is placed against the knuckles. While a broken finger will not stop an attacker dead in his tracks, it's a very effective target when breaking free from holds. Remember that a broken finger cannot maintain the structural integrity of a grip. This is particularly important when fighting a grappler in a ground fight. The fingers can be bitten, broken, torn and in some cases, punched.

Here, the author demonstrates a finger tear technique used to escape from a full-nelson hold.

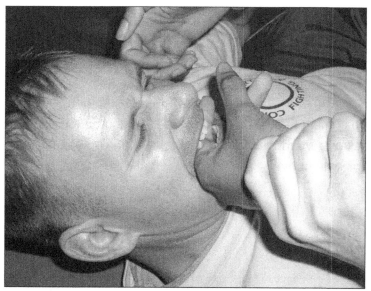

The fingers are especially vulnerable to biting.

139

Toes

In grappling range, a powerful stomp of your heel can break the small bones of the assailant's toes, causing severe pain and immediate immobility. Stomping on the assailant's toes is also one of the best ways for releasing many holds. Keep in mind that you should avoid attacking the toes if the attacker is wearing hard leather boots, (i.e., combat, hiking or motorcycle boots).

Pictured here, the foot stomp.

CHAPTER FOUR
Advanced Pressure Point Fighting

Razing

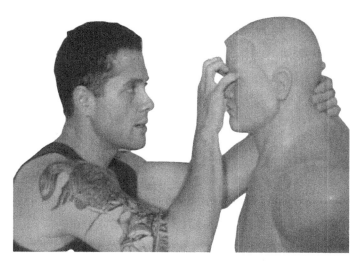

Now that we've covered all of the pressure point targets, it's time to show you how to attack all of them in one vicious overwhelming assault called *Razing*. This advanced form of pressure point fighting comes from my WidowMaker Program.

In Contemporary Fighting Arts, razing is a series of vicious close-quarter techniques designed to physically and psychologically destroy a criminal attacker. These close-quarter techniques are executed at various beats, and they include the following techniques:

- **Eye rakes**
- **Eyes gouges**
- **Tearing**
- **Throat crushing**
- **Biting**
- **Elbow Strikes**

- **Hair Pulling**
- **Head Butts**
- **Biceps pops**
- **Palm jolts**
- **Neck cranks**
- **Finishing chokes**

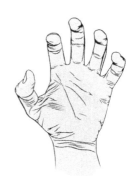

I've been teaching reality based self-defense (RBSD) for over thirty years and I can say, with one-hundred percent confidence, that razing is the most devastating form of unarmed fighting know to man. Its brutal and invasive characteristics are both physically and psychologically traumatic for the recipient. The overwhelming nature of razing invokes instantaneous panic by delivering a destructiveness exceeding that of a deadly and evil criminal aggressor.

When razing is properly performed, it accomplishes the following objectives:

1. Cognitive Brain Shutdown - The brutal and overwhelming nature of razing overrides the opponent's cognitive brain preventing him from any lucid thought process. Since razing is so fast and ferocious, the opponent's cognitive brain can't process what is happening to him.

2. Instant Damage - Razing is simply indefensible! The speed and proximity at which these quarter beat hits are delivered is truly overwhelming. The bottom line is, they are just too fast and too close for the opponent to react defensively. In many ways, razing is likened to an angry swarm of wasps, your only hope is to try and escape from the pain.

Razing Demonstration

Step 1: Anchor the opponent's neck.

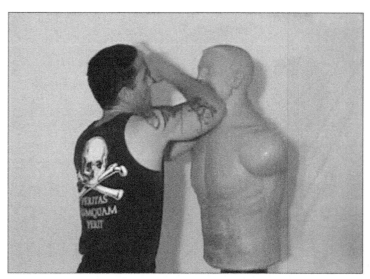

Step 2: Franco delivers a shaving forearm technique.

147

Step 3: He follows up with an eye rake.

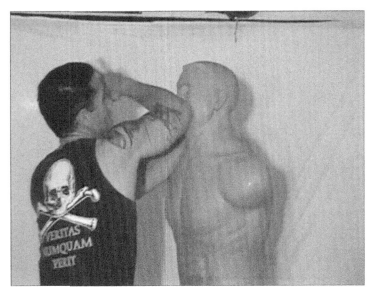
Step 4: Next, a shaving forearm.

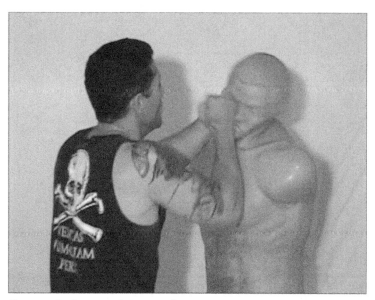

Step 5: A short arc hammer fist.

Step 6: Head butt.

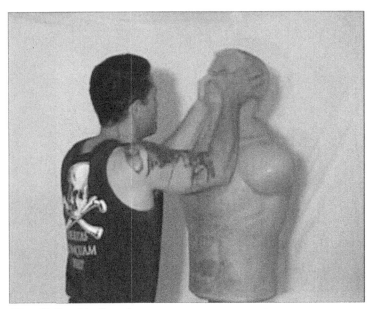

Step 7: Double thumb gouge.

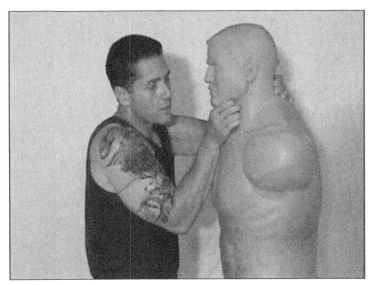

Step 8: Throat crush.

Step 9: Palm jolt.

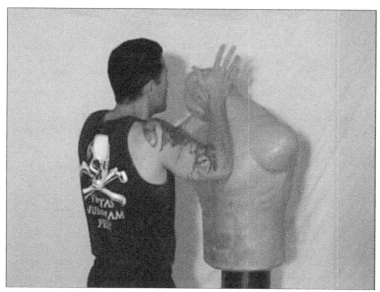

Step 10: Neck crank.

CHAPTER FIVE
Pressure Point Conditioning

Your Fate is in Your Hands!

Since 90% of pressure point techniques are delivered with your hands, it's important for you to strengthen your fingers, wrists and forearms. Powerful hands and forearms will amplify the power of your pressure point strikes and help ensure victory in a fight. There are several effective hand and forearm exercises you can perform to strengthen these muscles.

What follows are several effective ways to condition and strengthen your hands, wrists and forearms.

Power Putty

One excellent hand exerciser that strengthens all the muscles in your fingers and hands is Power Putty. Essentially, Power Putty is a flexible silicone rubber that can be squeezed, stretched, and crushed. Begin using the putty for ten minute sessions and progressively build up to thirty minutes. Remember to work both hands equally.

Hand Grippers

Another effective way to strengthen your hands, wrists and forearms is to work out with heavy duty hand grippers. While there are a wide selection of them on the market, I personally prefer using the Captains of Crush brand. These high quality grippers are virtually indestructible and they are sold in a variety of different resistance levels ranging from 60 to 365 pounds.

IronMind EGG

This is another great tool for strengthening and conditioning your hands. Made of a 21st century polymer, the IronMind EGG will add a new dimension to your grip training.

Tennis Ball

If you are low on cash and just starting out with your training, you can begin by squeezing a tennis ball a couple times per week. One hundred repetitions per hand would be a great start.

Weight Training

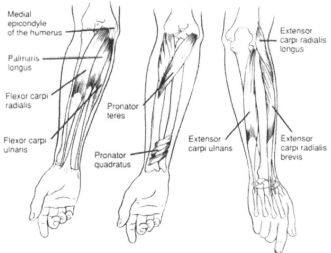

Medial
epicondyle
of the humerus

Palmaris
longus

Flexor carpi
radialis

Pronator
teres

Flexor carpi
ulnaris

Pronator
quadratus

Extensor
carpi ulnaris

Extensor
carpi radialis
longus

Extensor
carpi radialis
brevis

Finally, you can also condition your wrists and forearms by performing various forearm exercises with free weights. Exercises like: hammer curls, reverse curls, wrist curls, and reverse wrist curls are great for developing powerful forearms. When training your forearms, be certain to work both your extensor and flexor muscles. Let's look at some of the exercises.

Barbell Wrist Curls

This exercise strengthens the flexor muscles. Perform 5 sets of 8-10 repetitions. To perform the exercise, follow these steps:

1. Sit at the end of a bench, grab a barbell with an underhand grip and place both of your hands close together.

2. In a smooth and controlled fashion, slowly bend your wrists and lower the barbell toward the floor.

3. Contract your forearms and curl the weight back to the starting position.

Reverse Wrist Curls

This exercise develops and strengthens the extensor muscle of the forearm. Perform 6 sets of 6-8 repetitions. To perform the exercise, follow these steps:

1. Sit at the end of a bench, hold a barbell with an overhand grip (your hands should be approximately 11 inches apart) and place your forearms on top of your thighs.

2. Slowly lower the barbell as far as your wrists will allow.

3. Flex your wrists upward back to the starting position.

Behind-the-Back Wrist Curls

This exercise strengthens both the flexor muscles of the forearms. Perform 5 sets of 6-8 repetitions To perform the exercise, follow these steps:

1. Hold a barbell behind your back at arm's length (your hands should be approximately shoulder-width apart).

2. Uncurl your finger and let the barbell slowly roll down your palms.

3. Close your hands and roll the barbell back into your hands.

Hammer Curls

This exercise strengthens both the Brachialis and Brachioradialis muscles. Perform 5 sets of 8-10 repetitions. To perform the exercise, follow these steps:

1. Stand with both feet approximately shoulder width apart, with both dumbbells at your sides.

2. Keeping your elbows close to your body and your palms facing inward, slowly curl both dumbbells upward towards your shoulders.

3. Slowly return to the starting position.

Reverse Barbell Curls

Reverse curls can be a great alternative to hammer curls. This exercise strengthens both the Brachialis and Brachioradialis muscles. Perform 5 sets of 8-10 repetitions. To perform the exercise, follow these steps:

1. Stand with both feet approximately shoulder width apart. Hold a barbell with your palms facing down (pronated grip).

2. Keeping your upper arms stationary, curl the weights up until the bar is at shoulder level.

3. Slowly return to the starting position.

General Combat Conditioning

Finally, if you want to maximize the efficiency and effectiveness of your fighting skills, you must be physically fit. Fitness and conditioning comprises the following three broad components: cardiorespiratory conditioning, muscular/ skeletal conditioning, and proper body composition.

The cardiorespiratory system includes the heart, lungs, and circulatory system, which undergo tremendous stress in a high-risk situation. So you're going to have to run, jog, bike, swim, or skip rope to develop sound cardiorespiratory conditioning. Each aerobic workout should last a minimum of 30 minutes and be performed at least four times per week.

The second component of conditioning is muscular/skeletal conditioning. To strengthen your bones and muscles to withstand the rigors of combat, your training must include progressive resistance (weight training). You will also need a stretching program designed to loosen up every muscle group. As I said earlier, stretching on a regular basis will also increase the muscles' range of motion, improve circulation, reduce the possibility of injury and relieve daily stress.

The final component of conditioning is proper body composition: simply, the ratio of fat to lean body tissue. Your diet and training regimen will affect your level or percentage of body fat significantly. A sensible and consistent exercise program accompanied by a healthy and balanced diet will facilitate proper body composition.

Appendix A

What follows is a list of ineffectual pressure point targets that will yield poor results in unarmed combat. This list doesn't apply to armed combat (i.e., firearms, edged weapons, etc).

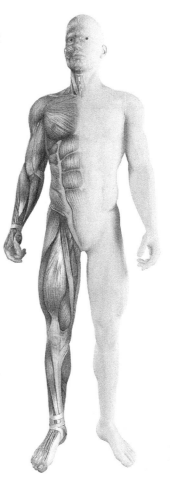

- Coronal Suture (the two frontal and parietal bones)
- Mastoid
- Sternocleidomastoid regic
- Brachial Plexus
- Trapezius muscle
- Spleen
- Kidneys
- Bladder
- Biceps
- Elbow
- Radial nerve
- Heart
- Abdominal muscles
- Coccyx
- Gastrocnemius muscle
- Achilles tendon

Glossary of Terms

The following terms are defined in the context of Contemporary Fighting Arts and its related concepts. In many instances, the definitions bear little resemblance to those found in a standard dictionary.

A

accuracy—The precise or exact projection of force. Accuracy is also defined as the ability to execute a combative movement with precision and exactness.

adaptabllity—The ability to physically and psychologically adjust to new or different conditions or circumstances of combat.

advanced first-strike tools—Offensive techniques that are specifically used when confronted with multiple opponents.

aerobic exercise—Literally, "with air." Exercise that elevates the heart rate to a training level for a prolonged period of time, usually 30 minutes.

affective preparedness – One of the three components of preparedness. Affective preparedness means being emotionally, philosophically, and spiritually prepared for the strains of combat. See cognitive preparedness and psychomotor preparedness.

aggression—Hostile and injurious behavior directed toward a person.

aggressive response—One of the three possible counters when assaulted by a grab, choke, or hold from a standing position. Aggressive response requires you to counter the enemy with destructive blows and strikes. See moderate response and passive response.

aggressive hand positioning—Placement of hands so as to imply aggressive or hostile intentions.

agility—An attribute of combat. One's ability to move his or her body quickly and gracefully.

amalgamation—A scientific process of uniting or merging.

ambidextrous—The ability to perform with equal facility on both the right and left sides of the body.

anabolic steroids – synthetic chemical compounds that resemble the male sex hormone testosterone. This performance-enhancing drug is known to increase lean muscle mass, strength, and endurance.

analysis and integration—One of the five elements of CFA's mental component. This is the painstaking process of breaking down various elements, concepts, sciences, and disciplines into their atomic parts, and then methodically and strategically analyzing, experimenting, and drastically modifying the information so that it fulfills three combative requirements: efficiency, effectiveness, and safety. Only then is it finally integrated into the CFA system.

anatomical striking targets—The various anatomical body targets that can be struck and which are especially vulnerable to potential harm. They include: the eyes, temple, nose, chin, back of neck, front of neck, solar plexus, ribs, groin, thighs, knees, shins, and instep.

anchoring – The strategic process of trapping the assailant's neck or limb in order to control the range of engagement during razing.

assailant—A person who threatens or attacks another person.

assault—The threat or willful attempt to inflict injury

upon the person of another.

assault and battery—The unlawful touching of another person without justification.

assessment—The process of rapidly gathering, analyzing, and accurately evaluating information in terms of threat and danger. You can assess people, places, actions, and objects.

attack—Offensive action designed to physically control, injure, or kill another person.

attack by combination (ABC) - One of the five methods of attack. See compound attack.

attack by drawing (ABD) - One of the five methods of attack. A method of attack predicated on counterattack.

attitude—Attitude means being emotionally, philosophically, and spiritually liberated from societal and religious mores. See skills and knowledge.

attributes of combat—The physical, mental, and spiritual qualities that enhance combat skills and tactics.

awareness—Perception or knowledge of people, places, actions, and objects. (In CFA, there are three categories of tactical awareness: criminal awareness, situational awareness, and self-awareness.)

B

balance—One's ability to maintain equilibrium while stationary or moving.

blading the body—Strategically positioning your body at a 45-degree angle.

blitz and disengage—A style of sparring whereby a

fighter moves into a range of combat, unleashes a strategic compound attack, and then quickly disengages to a safe distance. Of all sparring methodologies, the blitz and disengage most closely resembles a real street fight.

block—A defensive tool designed to intercept the assailant's attack by placing a non-vital target between the assailant's strike and your vital body target.

body composition—The ratio of fat to lean body tissue.

body language—Nonverbal communication through posture, gestures, and facial expressions.

body mechanics—Technically precise body movement during the execution of a body weapon, defensive technique, or other fighting maneuver.

body tackle – A tackle that occurs when your opponent haphazardly rushes forward and plows his body into yours.

body weapon—Also known as a tool, one of the various body parts that can be used to strike or otherwise injure or kill a criminal assailant.

burn out—A negative emotional state acquired by physically over- training. Some symptoms include: illness, boredom, anxiety, disinterest in training, and general sluggishness.

C

cadence—Coordinating tempo and rhythm to establish a timing pattern of movement.

cardiorespiratory conditioning—The component of physical fitness that deals with the heart, lungs, and circulatory system.

centerline—An imaginary vertical line that divides your body in half and which contains many of your vital anatomical targets.

choke holds—Holds that impair the flow of blood or oxygen to the brain.

circular movements—Movements that follow the direction of a curve.

close-quarter combat—One of the three ranges of knife and bludgeon combat. At this distance, you can strike, slash, or stab your assailant with a variety of close-quarter techniques.

cognitive development—One of the five elements of CFA's mental component. The process of developing and enhancing your fighting skills through specific mental exercises and techniques. See analysis and integration, killer instinct, philosophy, and strategic/tactical development.

cognitive exercises—Various mental exercises used to enhance fighting skills and tactics.

cognitive preparedness – One of the three components of preparedness. Cognitive preparedness means being equipped with the strategic concepts, principles, and general knowledge of combat. See affective preparedness and psychomotor preparedness.

combat-oriented training—Training that is specifically related to the harsh realities of both armed and unarmed combat. See ritual-oriented training and sport-oriented training.

combative arts—The various arts of war. See martial arts.

combative attributes—See attributes of combat.

combative fitness—A state characterized by cardiorespiratory and muscular/skeletal conditioning, as well as proper body composition.

combative mentality—Also known as the killer instinct, this is a combative state of mind necessary for fighting. See killer instinct.

combat ranges—The various ranges of unarmed combat.

combative utility—The quality of condition of being combatively useful.

combination(s)—See compound attack.

common peroneal nerve—A pressure point area located approximately four to six inches above the knee on the midline of the outside of the thigh.

composure—A combative attribute. Composure is a quiet and focused mind-set that enables you to acquire your combative agenda.

compound attack—One of the five conventional methods of attack. Two or more body weapons launched in strategic succession whereby the fighter overwhelms his assailant with a flurry of full speed, full-force blows.

conditioning training—A CFA training methodology requiring the practitioner to deliver a variety of offensive and defensive combinations for a 4-minute period. See proficiency training and street training.

contact evasion—Physically moving or manipulating your body to avoid being tackled by the adversary.

Contemporary Fighting Arts—A modern martial art and self-defense system made up of three parts: physical, mental, and spiritual.

conventional ground-fighting tools—Specific ground-fighting techniques designed to control, restrain, and temporarily incapacitate your adversary. Some conventional ground fighting tactics include: submission holds, locks, certain choking techniques, and specific striking techniques.

coordination—A physical attribute characterized by the ability to perform a technique or movement with efficiency, balance, and accuracy.

counterattack—Offensive action made to counter an assailant's initial attack.

courage—A combative attribute. The state of mind and spirit that enables a fighter to face danger and vicissitudes with confidence, resolution, and bravery.

creatine monohydrate—A tasteless and odorless white powder that mimics some of the effects of anabolic steroids. Creatine is a safe body-building product that can benefit anyone who wants to increase their strength, endurance, and lean muscle mass.

criminal awareness—One of the three categories of CFA awareness. It involves a general understanding and knowledge of the nature and dynamics of a criminal's motivations, mentalities, methods, and capabilities to perpetrate violent crime. See situational awareness and self-awareness.

criminal justice—The study of criminal law and the procedures associated with its enforcement.

criminology—The scientific study of crime and criminals.

cross-stepping—The process of crossing one foot in front of or behind the other when moving.

crushing tactics—Nuclear grappling-range techniques

designed to crush the assailant's anatomical targets.

D

deadly force—Weapons or techniques that may result in unconsciousness, permanent disfigurement, or death.

deception—A combative attribute. A stratagem whereby you delude your assailant.

decisiveness—A combative attribute. The ability to follow a tactical course of action that is unwavering and focused.

defense—The ability to strategically thwart an assailant's attack (armed or unarmed).

defensive flow—A progression of continuous defensive responses.

defensive mentality—A defensive mind-set.

defensive reaction time—The elapsed time between an assailant's physical attack and your defensive response to that attack. See offensive reaction time.

demeanor—A person's outward behavior. One of the essential factors to consider when assessing a threatening individual.

diet—A lifestyle of healthy eating.

disingenuous vocalization—The strategic and deceptive utilization of words to successfully launch a preemptive strike at your adversary.

distancing—The ability to quickly understand spatial relationships and how they relate to combat.

distractionary tactics—Various verbal and physical tactics designed to distract your adversary.

double-end bag—A small leather ball hung from the ceiling and anchored to the floor with bungee cord. It helps develop striking accuracy, speed, timing, eye-hand coordination, footwork and overall defensive skills.

double-leg takedown—A takedown that occurs when your opponent shoots for both of your legs to force you to the ground.

E

ectomorph—One of the three somatotypes. A body type characterized by a high degree of slenderness, angularity, and fragility. See endomorph and mesomorph.

effectiveness—One of the three criteria for a CFA body weapon, technique, tactic, or maneuver. It means the ability to produce a desired effect. See efficiency and safety.

efficiency—One of the three criteria for a CFA body weapon, technique, tactic, or maneuver. It means the ability to reach an objective quickly and economically. See effectiveness and safety.

emotionless—A combative attribute. Being temporarily devoid of human feeling.

endomorph—One of the three somatotypes. A body type characterized by a high degree of roundness, softness, and body fat. See ectomorph and mesomorph.

evasion—A defensive maneuver that allows you to strategically maneuver your body away from the assailant's strike.

evasive sidestepping—Evasive footwork where the practitioner moves to either the right or left side.

evasiveness—A combative attribute. The ability to avoid threat or danger.

excessive force—An amount of force that exceeds the need for a particular event and is unjustified in the eyes of the law.

experimentation—The painstaking process of testing a combative hypothesis or theory.

explosiveness—A combative attribute that is characterized by a sudden outburst of violent energy.

F

fear—A strong and unpleasant emotion caused by the anticipation or awareness of threat or danger. There are three stages of fear in order of intensity: fright, panic, and terror. See fright, panic, and terror.

feeder—A skilled technician who holds and manipulates the focus mitts.

femoral nerve—A pressure point area located approximately 6 inches above the knee on the inside of the thigh.

fighting stance—Any one of the stances used in CFA's system. A strategic posture you can assume when face-to-face with an unarmed assailant(s). The fighting stance is generally used after you have launched your first-strike tool.

fight-or-flight syndrome—A response of the sympathetic nervous system to a fearful and threatening situation, during which it prepares your body to either fight or flee from the perceived danger.

finesse—A combative attribute. The ability to skillfully execute a movement or a series of movements with grace and refinement.

first strike—Proactive force used to interrupt the initial stages of an assault before it becomes a self-defense situation.

first-strike principle—A CFA principle that states that when physical danger is imminent and you have no other tactical option but to fight back, you should strike first, strike fast, and strike with authority and keep the pressure on.

first-strike stance—One of the stances used in CFA's system. A strategic posture used prior to initiating a first strike.

first-strike tools—Specific offensive tools designed to initiate a preemptive strike against your adversary.

fisted blows – Hand blows delivered with a clenched fist.

five tactical options – The five strategic responses you can make in a self-defense situation, listed in order of increasing level of resistance: comply, escape, de-escalate, assert, and fight back.

flexibility—The muscles' ability to move through maximum natural ranges. See muscular/skeletal conditioning.
focus mitts—Durable leather hand mitts used to develop and sharpen offensive and defensive skills.

footwork—Quick, economical steps performed on the balls of the feet while you are relaxed, alert, and balanced. Footwork is structured around four general movements: forward, backward, right, and left.

fractal tool—Offensive or defensive tools that can be used in more than one combat range.

fright—The first stage of fear; quick and sudden fear. See panic and terror.

full beat – One of the four beat classifications in the Widow Maker Program. The full beat strike has a complete initiation and retraction phase.

G

going postal - a slang term referring to a person who suddenly and unexpectedly attacks you with an explosive and frenzied flurry of blows. Also known as postal attack.

grappling range—One of the three ranges of unarmed combat. Grappling range is the closest distance of unarmed combat from which you can employ a wide variety of close-quarter tools and techniques. The grappling range of unarmed combat is also divided into two planes: vertical (standing) and horizontal (ground fighting). See kicking range and punching range.

grappling-range tools—The various body tools and techniques that are employed in the grappling range of unarmed combat, including head butts; biting, tearing, clawing, crushing, and gouging tactics; foot stomps, horizontal, vertical, and diagonal elbow strikes, vertical and diagonal knee strikes, chokes, strangles, joint locks, and holds. See punching range tools and kicking range tools.

ground fighting—Also known as the horizontal grappling plane, this is fighting that takes place on the ground.

guard—Also known as the hand guard, this refers to a fighter's hand positioning.

guard position—Also known as leg guard or scissors hold, this is a ground-fighting position in which a fighter is on his back holding his opponent between his legs.

H

half beat – One of the four beat classifications in the Widow Maker Program. The half beat strike is delivered through the retraction phase of the proceeding strike.

hand immobilization attack (HIA) - One of the five methods of attack. A method of attack whereby the practitioner traps his opponent's limb or limbs in order to execute an offense attack of his own.

hand positioning —See guard.

hand wraps—Long strips of cotton that are wrapped around the hands and wrists for greater protection.

haymaker—A wild and telegraphed swing of the arms executed by an unskilled fighter.

head-hunter—A fighter who primarily attacks the head.

heavy bag—A large cylindrical bag used to develop kicking, punching, or striking power.

high-line kick—One of the two different classifications of a kick. A kick that is directed to targets above an assailant's waist level. See low-line kick.

hip fusing—A full-contact drill that teaches a fighter to "stand his ground" and overcome the fear of exchanging blows with a stronger opponent. This exercise is performed by connecting two fighters with a 3-foot chain, forcing them to fight in the punching range of unarmed combat.

histrionics—The field of theatrics or acting.

hook kick—A circular kick that can be delivered in both

kicking and punching ranges.

hook punch—A circular punch that can be delivered in both the punching and grappling ranges.

I

impact power—Destructive force generated by mass and velocity.

impact training—A training exercise that develops pain tolerance.

incapacitate—To disable an assailant by rendering him unconscious or damaging his bones, joints, or organs.

initiative—Making the first offensive move in combat.

inside position—The area between the opponent's arms, where he has the greatest amount of control.

intent—One of the essential factors to consider when assessing a threatening individual. The assailant's purpose or motive. See demeanor, positioning, range, and weapon capability.

intuition—The innate ability to know or sense something without the use of rational thought.

J

jeet kune do (JKD) - "Way of the intercepting fist." Bruce Lee's approach to the martial arts, which includes his innovative concepts, theories, methodologies, and philosophies.

jersey Pull – Strategically pulling the assailant's shirt or jacket over his head as he disengages from the clinch position.

joint lock—A grappling-range technique that immobilizes the assailant's joint.

K

kick—A sudden, forceful strike with the foot.

kicking range—One of the three ranges of unarmed combat. Kicking range is the furthest distance of unarmed combat wherein you use your legs to strike an assailant. See grappling range and punching range.

kicking-range tools—The various body weapons employed in the kicking range of unarmed combat, including side kicks, push kicks, hook kicks, and vertical kicks.

killer instinct—A cold, primal mentality that surges to your consciousness and turns you into a vicious fighter.

kinesics—The study of nonlinguistic body movement communications. (For example, eye movement, shrugs, or facial gestures.)

kinesiology—The study of principles and mechanics of human movement.

kinesthetic perception—The ability to accurately feel your body during the execution of a particular movement.

knowledge—One of the three factors that determine who will win a street fight. Knowledge means knowing and understanding how to fight. See skills and attitude.

L

lead side -The side of the body that faces an assailant.

leg guard—See guard position.

linear movement—Movements that follow the path of a straight line.

low-maintenance tool—Offensive and defensive tools that require the least amount of training and practice to maintain proficiency. Low maintenance tools generally do not require preliminary stretching.

low-line kick—One of the two different classifications of a kick. A kick that is directed to targets below the assailant's waist level. (See high-line kick.)

lock—See joint lock.

M

maneuver—To manipulate into a strategically desired position.

MAP—An acronym that stands for moderate, aggressive, passive. MAP provides the practitioner with three possible responses to various grabs, chokes, and holds that occur from a standing position. See aggressive response, moderate response, and passive response.

martial arts—The "arts of war."

masking—The process of concealing your true feelings from your opponent by manipulating and managing your body language.

mechanics—(See body mechanics.)

mental attributes—The various cognitive qualities that enhance your fighting skills.

mental component—One of the three vital components of the CFA system. The mental component includes the cerebral aspects of fighting including the killer instinct, strategic and tactical development, analysis and integration, philosophy, and cognitive development. See physical component and spiritual component.

mesomorph—One of the three somatotypes. A body type classified by a high degree of muscularity and strength. The mesomorph possesses the ideal physique for unarmed combat. See ectomorph and endomorph.

mobility—A combative attribute. The ability to move your body quickly and freely while balanced. See footwork.

moderate response—One of the three possible counters when assaulted by a grab, choke, or hold from a standing position. Moderate response requires you to counter your opponent with a control and restraint (submission hold). See aggressive response and passive response.

modern martial art—A pragmatic combat art that has evolved to meet the demands and characteristics of the present time.

mounted position—A dominant ground-fighting position where a fighter straddles his opponent.

muscular endurance—The muscles' ability to perform the same motion or task repeatedly for a prolonged period of time.

muscular flexibility—The muscles' ability to move through maximum natural ranges.

muscular strength—The maximum force that can be

exerted by a particular muscle or muscle group against resistance.

muscular/skeletal conditioning—An element of physical fitness that entails muscular strength, endurance, and flexibility.

N

naked choke—A throat choke executed from the chest to back position. This secure choke is executed with two hands and it can be performed while standing, kneeling, and ground fighting with the opponent.

neck crush – A powerful pain compliance technique used when the adversary buries his head in your chest to avoid being razed.

neutralize—See incapacitate.

neutral zone—The distance outside the kicking range at which neither the practitioner nor the assailant can touch the other.

nonaggressive physiology—Strategic body language used prior to initiating a first strike.

non-telegraphic movement—Body mechanics or movements that do not inform an assailant of your intentions.

nuclear ground-fighting tools—Specific grappling range tools designed to inflict immediate and irreversible damage. Nuclear tools and tactics include biting tactics, tearing tactics, crushing tactics, continuous choking tactics, gouging techniques, raking tactics, and all striking techniques.

O

offense—The armed and unarmed means and methods of attacking a criminal assailant.

offensive flow—Continuous offensive movements (kicks, blows, and strikes) with unbroken continuity that ultimately neutralize or terminate the opponent. See compound attack.

offensive reaction time—The elapsed time between target selection and target impaction.

one-mindedness—A state of deep concentration wherein you are free from all distractions (internal and external).

ostrich defense—One of the biggest mistakes one can make when defending against an opponent. This is when the practitioner looks away from that which he fears (punches, kicks, and strikes). His mentality is, "If I can't see it, it can't hurt me."

P

pain tolerance—Your ability to physically and psychologically withstand pain.

panic—The second stage of fear; overpowering fear. See fright and terror.

parry—A defensive technique: a quick, forceful slap that redirects an assailant's linear attack. There are two types of parries: horizontal and vertical.

passive response—One of the three possible counters when assaulted by a grab, choke, or hold from a standing position. Passive response requires you to nullify the assault without injuring your adversary. See aggressive response and moderate response.

patience—A combative attribute. The ability to endure and tolerate difficulty.

perception—Interpretation of vital information acquired from your senses when faced with a potentially threatening situation.

philosophical resolution—The act of analyzing and answering various questions concerning the use of violence in defense of yourself and others.

philosophy—One of the five aspects of CFA's mental component. A deep state of introspection whereby you methodically resolve critical questions concerning the use of force in defense of yourself or others.

physical attributes—The numerous physical qualities that enhance your combative skills and abilities.

physical component—One of the three vital components of the CFA system. The physical component includes the physical aspects of fighting, such as physical fitness, weapon/technique mastery, and combative attributes. See mental component and spiritual component.

physical conditioning—See combative fitness.

physical fitness—See combative fitness.

positional asphyxia—The arrangement, placement, or positioning of your opponent's body in such a way as to interrupt your breathing and cause unconsciousness or possibly death.

positioning—The spatial relationship of the assailant to the assailed person in terms of target exposure, escape, angle of attack, and various other strategic considerations.

postal attack - see going postal.

power—A physical attribute of armed and unarmed combat. The amount of force you can generate when striking an anatomical target.

power generators—Specific points on your body that generate impact power. There are three anatomical power generators: shoulders, hips, and feet.

precision—See accuracy.

preemptive strike—See first strike.

premise—An axiom, concept, rule, or any other valid reason to modify or go beyond that which has been established.

preparedness—A state of being ready for combat. There are three components of preparedness: affective preparedness, cognitive preparedness, and psychomotor preparedness.

pressure point - a specific target on the human body that is especially vulnerable to attack. There are two types of pressure points: Pain compliance and Incapacitation.

probable reaction dynamics - The opponent's anticipated or predicted movements or actions during both armed and unarmed combat.

proficiency training—A CFA training methodology requiring the practitioner to execute a specific body weapon, technique, maneuver, or tactic over and over for a prescribed number of repetitions. See conditioning training and street training.

progressive indirect attack (PIA) – One of the five methods of attack. A progressive method of attack whereby the initial tool or technique is designed to set the opponent up for follow-up blows.

proxemics—The study of the nature and effect of man's personal space.

proximity—The ability to maintain a strategically safe distance from a threatening individual.

pseudospeciation—A combative attribute. The tendency to assign subhuman and inferior qualities to a threatening assailant.

psychological conditioning—The process of conditioning the mind for the horrors and rigors of real combat.

psychomotor preparedness—One of the three components of preparedness. Psychomotor preparedness means possessing all of the physical skills and attributes necessary to defeat a formidable adversary. See affective preparedness and cognitive preparedness.

punch—A quick, forceful strike of the fists.

punching range—One of the three ranges of unarmed combat. Punching range is the mid range of unarmed combat from which the fighter uses his hands to strike his assailant. See kicking range and grappling range.

punching-range tools—The various body weapons that are employed in the punching range of unarmed combat, including finger jabs, palm-heel strikes, rear cross, knife-hand strikes, horizontal and shovel hooks, uppercuts, and hammer-fist strikes. See grappling-range tools and kicking-range tools.

Q

qualities of combat—See attributes of combat.

quarter beat - One of the four beat classifications of the Widow Maker Program. Quarter beat strikes never break contact with the assailant's face. Quarter beat strikes are primarily responsible for creating the psychological panic and trauma when Razing.

R

range—The spatial relationship between a fighter and a threatening assailant.

range deficiency—The inability to effectively fight and defend in all ranges of combat (armed and unarmed).
range manipulation—A combative attribute. The strategic manipulation of combat ranges.

range proficiency—A combative attribute. The ability to effectively fight and defend in all ranges of combat (armed and unarmed).

ranges of engagement—See combat ranges.
ranges of unarmed combat—The three distances (kicking range, punching range, and grappling range) a fighter might physically engage with an assailant while involved in unarmed combat.

raze – To level, demolish or obliterate.

razer – One who performs the Razing methodology.

razing – The second phase of the Widow Maker Program. A series of vicious close quarter techniques designed to physically and psychologically extirpate a criminal attacker.

razing amplifier - a technique, tactic or procedure that magnifies the destructiveness of your razing technique.

reaction dynamics—see probable reaction dynamics.

reaction time—The elapsed time between a stimulus and the response to that particular stimulus. See offensive reaction time and defensive reaction time.

rear cross—A straight punch delivered from the rear hand that crosses from right to left (if in a left stance) or left to right (if in a right stance).

rear side—The side of the body furthest from the assailant. See lead side.

reasonable force—That degree of force which is not excessive for a particular event and which is appropriate in protecting yourself or others.

refinement—The strategic and methodical process of improving or perfecting.

relocation principle—Also known as relocating, this is a street-fighting tactic that requires you to immediately move to a new location (usually by flanking your adversary) after delivering a compound attack.

repetition—Performing a single movement, exercise, strike, or action continuously for a specific period.

research—A scientific investigation or inquiry.

rhythm—Movements characterized by the natural ebb and flow of related elements.

ritual-oriented training—Formalized training that is conducted without intrinsic purpose. See combat-oriented training and sport-oriented training.

S

safety—One of the three criteria for a CFA body

weapon, technique, maneuver, or tactic. It means that the tool, technique, maneuver or tactic provides the least amount of danger and risk for the practitioner. See efficiency and effectiveness.

scissors hold—See guard position.

scorching – Quickly and inconspicuously applying oleoresin capsicum (hot pepper extract) on your fingertips and then razing your adversary.

self-awareness—One of the three categories of CFA awareness. Knowing and understanding yourself. This includes aspects of yourself which may provoke criminal violence and which will promote a proper and strong reaction to an attack. See criminal awareness and situational awareness.

self-confidence—Having trust and faith in yourself.

self-enlightenment—The state of knowing your capabilities, limitations, character traits, feelings, general attributes, and motivations. See self-awareness.

set—A term used to describe a grouping of repetitions.

shadow fighting—A CFA training exercise used to develop and refine your tools, techniques, and attributes of armed and unarmed combat.

sharking – A counter attack technique that is used when your adversary grabs your razing hand shielding wedge - a defensive maneuver used to counter an unarmed postal attack.

simple direct attack (SDA) – One of the five methods of attack. A method of attack whereby the practitioner delivers a solitary offenses tool or technique. It may involve a series of discrete probes or one swift, powerful strike aimed at terminating the encounter.

situational awareness—One of the three categories of CFA awareness. A state of being totally alert to your immediate surroundings, including people, places, objects, and actions. (See criminal awareness and self-awareness.)

skeletal alignment—The proper alignment or arrangement of your body. Skeletal alignment maximizes the structural integrity of striking tools.

skills—One of the three factors that determine who will win a street fight. Skills refers to psychomotor proficiency with the tools and techniques of combat. See Attitude and Knowledge.

slipping—A defensive maneuver that permits you to avoid an assailant's linear blow without stepping out of range. Slipping can be accomplished by quickly snapping the head and upper torso sideways (right or left) to avoid the blow.

snap back—A defensive maneuver that permits you to avoid an assailant's linear and circular blows without stepping out of range. The snap back can be accomplished by quickly snapping the head backward to avoid the assailant's blow.

somatotypes—A method of classifying human body types or builds into three different categories: endomorph, mesomorph, and ectomorph. See endomorph, mesomorph, and ectomorph.

sparring—A training exercise where two or more fighters fight each other while wearing protective equipment.

speed—A physical attribute of armed and unarmed combat. The rate or a measure of the rapid rate of motion.

spiritual component—One of the three vital components of the CFA system. The spiritual component includes the metaphysical issues and aspects of existence. See physical component and mental component.

sport-oriented training—Training that is geared for competition and governed by a set of rules. See combat-oriented training and ritual-oriented training.

sprawling—A grappling technique used to counter a double- or single-leg takedown.

square off—To be face-to-face with a hostile or threatening assailant who is about to attack you.

stance—One of the many strategic postures you assume prior to or during armed or unarmed combat. stick fighting—Fighting that takes place with either one or two sticks.

strategic positioning—Tactically positioning yourself to either escape, move behind a barrier, or use a makeshift weapon.

strategic/tactical development—One of the five elements of CFA's mental component.

strategy—A carefully planned method of achieving your goal of engaging an assailant under advantageous conditions.
street fight—A spontaneous and violent confrontation between two or more individuals wherein no rules apply.

street fighter—An unorthodox combatant who has no formal training. His combative skills and tactics are usually developed in the street by the process of trial and error.

street training—A CFA training methodology requiring the practitioner to deliver explosive compound attacks for 10 to 20 seconds. See conditioning training and proficiency training.

strength training—The process of developing muscular strength through systematic application of progressive resistance.

striking art—A combat art that relies predominantly on striking techniques to neutralize or terminate a criminal attacker.

striking shield—A rectangular shield constructed of foam and vinyl used to develop power in your kicks, punches, and strikes.

striking tool—A natural body weapon that impacts with the assailant's anatomical target.

strong side—The strongest and most coordinated side of your body.

structure—A definite and organized pattern.

style—The distinct manner in which a fighter executes or performs his combat skills.

stylistic integration—The purposeful and scientific collection of tools and techniques from various disciplines, which are strategically integrated and dramatically altered to meet three essential criteria: efficiency, effectiveness, and combative safety.

submission holds—Also known as control and restraint techniques, many of these locks and holds create sufficient pain to cause the adversary to submit.

system—The unification of principles, philosophies, rules, strategies, methodologies, tools, and techniques of a particular method of combat.

T

tactic—The skill of using the available means to achieve an end.

target awareness—A combative attribute that encompasses five strategic principles: target orientation, target recognition, target selection, target impaction, and target exploitation.

target exploitation—A combative attribute. The strategic maximization of your assailant's reaction dynamics during a fight. Target exploitation can be applied in both armed and unarmed encounters.

target impaction—The successful striking of the appropriate anatomical target.

target orientation—A combative attribute. Having a workable knowledge of the assailant's anatomical targets.

target recognition—The ability to immediately recognize appropriate anatomical targets during an emergency self-defense situation.

target selection—The process of mentally selecting the appropriate anatomical target for your self-defense situation. This is predicated on certain factors, including proper force response, assailant's positioning, and range.

target stare—A form of telegraphing in which you stare at the anatomical target you intend to strike.

target zones—The three areas in which an assailant's anatomical targets are located. (See zone one, zone two and zone three.)

technique—A systematic procedure by which a task is

accomplished.

telegraphic cognizance—A combative attribute. The ability to recognize both verbal and non-verbal signs of aggression or assault.

telegraphing—Unintentionally making your intentions known to your adversary.

tempo—The speed or rate at which you speak.

terror—The third stage of fear; defined as overpowering fear. See fright and panic.

timing—A physical and mental attribute of armed and unarmed combat. Your ability to execute a movement at the optimum moment.

tone—The overall quality or character of your voice.

tool—See body weapon.

traditional martial arts—Any martial art that fails to evolve and change to meet the demands and characteristics of its present environment.

traditional style/system—See traditional martial arts. training drills—The various exercises and drills aimed at perfecting combat skills, attributes, and tactics.

trap and tuck – A counter move technique used when the adversary attempts to raze you during your quarter beat assault.

U

unified mind—A mind free and clear of distractions and focused on the combative situation.

use of force response—A combative attribute.

Selecting the appropriate level of force for a particular emergency self-defense situation.

V

viciousness—A combative attribute. The propensity to be extremely violent and destructive often characterized by intense savagery.

violence—The intentional utilization of physical force to coerce, injure, cripple, or kill.

visualization—Also known as mental visualization or mental imagery. The purposeful formation of mental images and scenarios in the mind's eye.

W

warm-up—A series of mild exercises, stretches, and movements designed to prepare you for more intense exercise.

weak side—The weaker and more uncoordinated side of your body.

weapon and technique mastery—A component of CFA's physical component. The kinesthetic and psychomotor development of a weapon or combative technique.

weapon capability—An assailant's ability to use and attack with a particular weapon.

webbing - The first phase of the Widow Maker Program. Webbing is a two hand strike delivered to the assailant's chin. It is called Webbing because your hands resemble a large web that wraps around the enemy's face.

widow maker – One who makes widows by destroying

husbands.

widow maker program – A CFA combat program specifically designed to teach the law abiding citizen how to use extreme force when faced with immediate threat of unlawful deadly criminal attack. The Widow Maker program is divided into two phases or methodologies: Webbing and Razing.

Y

yell—A loud and aggressive scream or shout used for various strategic reasons.

Z

zero beat – One of the four beat classifications of the Widow Maker, Feral Fighting and Savage Street Fighting Programs. Zero beat strikes are full pressure techniques applied to a specific target until it completely ruptures. They include gouging, crushing, biting, and choking techniques.

zone one—Anatomical targets related to your senses, including the eyes, temple, nose, chin, and back of neck.

zone three—Anatomical targets related to your mobility, including thighs, knees, shins, and instep.

zone two—Anatomical targets related to your breathing, including front of neck, solar plexus, ribs, and groin.

Additional Resources

You can find books and videos related to topics discussed in this book by visiting us at: ContemporaryFightingArts.com

Suggested Books:

1. The WidowMaker Program: *Extreme Self-Defense for Deadly Force Situations*

2. First Strike: *End A Fight in Ten Seconds or Less*

3. Knockout: *The Ultimate Guide to Sucker Punching*

4. Kubotan Power: *Quick and Simple Steps to Mastering The Kubotan Keychain*

Suggested Videos:

1. Pressure Point Fighting

2. Choke Out

3. First Strike

4. The WidowMaker Program

5. Kubotan Self-Defense

About Sammy Franco

With over 30 years of experience, Sammy Franco is one of the world's foremost authorities on armed and unarmed self- defense. Highly regarded as a leading innovator in combat sciences, Mr.

Franco was one of the premier pioneers in the field of "reality- based" self-defense and martial arts instruction.

Sammy Franco is perhaps best known as the founder and creator of Contemporary Fighting Arts (CFA), a state-of-the-art offensive- based combat system that is specifically designed for real-world self- defense. CFA is a sophisticated and practical system of self-defense, designed specifically to provide efficient and effective methods to avoid, defuse, confront, and neutralize both armed and unarmed attackers.

Sammy Franco has frequently been featured in martial art magazines, newspapers, and appeared on numerous radio and television programs. Mr. Franco has also authored numerous books, magazine articles, and editorials, and has developed a popular library of instructional videos.

Sammy Franco's experience and credibility in the combat sciences is unequaled. One of his many accomplishments in this field includes the fact that he has earned the ranking of a Law Enforcement Master Instructor, and has designed, implemented, and taught officer survival training to the United States Border Patrol (USBP). He has instructed members of the US Secret Service, Military Special Forces,

Washington DC Police Department, Montgomery County, Maryland Deputy Sheriffs, and the US Library of Congress Police. Sammy Franco is also a member of the prestigious International Law Enforcement Educators and Trainers Association (ILEETA) as well as the American Society of Law Enforcement Trainers (ASLET) and he is listed in the "Who's Who Director of Law Enforcement Instructors."

Sammy Franco is a nationally certified Law Enforcement Instructor in the following curricula: PR-24 Side-Handle Baton, Police Arrest and Control Procedures, Police Personal Weapons Tactics, Police Power Handcuffing Methods, Police Oleoresin Capsicum Aerosol Training (OCAT), Police Weapon Retention and Disarming Methods, Police Edged Weapon Countermeasures and "Use of Force" Assessment and Response Methods.

Mr. Franco holds a Bachelor of Arts degree in Criminal Justice from the University of Maryland. He is a regularly featured speaker at a number of professional conferences and conducts dynamic and enlightening seminars on numerous aspects of self-defense and combat training.

On a personal level, Sammy Franco is an animal lover, who will go to great lengths to assist and rescue animals. Throughout the years, he's rescued everything from turkey vultures to goats. However, his most treasured moments are always spent with his beloved German Shepherd dogs.

For more information about Mr. Franco, you can visit his website at: **ContemporaryFightingArts.com** or follow him on twitter @**RealSammyFranco**

Other Books by Sammy Franco

THE WIDOW MAKER PROGRAM
Extreme Self-Defense for
Deadly Force Situations
by Sammy Franco

In The Widow Maker Program is a shocking and revolutionary fighting style designed to unleash extreme force when faced with the immediate threat of an unlawful deadly criminal attack. In this unique book, self-defense innovator Sammy Franco teaches you his brutal and unorthodox combat style that is virtually indefensible and utterly devastating. With over 250 photographs and detailed step-by-step instructions, The Widow Maker Program teaches you Franco's surreptitious Webbing and Razing techniques. When combined, these two fighting methods create an unstoppable force capable of destroying the toughest adversary. 8.5 x 5.5, paperback, photos, illus, 218 pages.

WAR MACHINE
How to Transform Yourself Into A Vicious & Deadly
Street Fighter
by Sammy Franco

War Machine is a book that will change you for the rest of your life! When followed accordingly, War Machine will forge your mind, body and spirit into iron. Once armed with the mental and physical attributes of the War Machine, you will become a strong and confident warrior that can handle just about anything that life may throw your way. In essence, War Machine is a way of life. Powerful, intense, and hard. 11 x 8.5, paperback, photos, illustrations, 210 pages

CANE FIGHTING
The Authoritative Guide to Using the Cane or Walking Stick for Self-Defense
by Sammy Franco

Cane Fighting: The Authoritative Guide to Using the Cane or Walking Stick for Self-Defense is a no nonsense book written for anyone who wants to learn how to use the cane or walking stick as a fighting weapon for real-world self-defense. With over 200 photographs and step-by-step instructions, Cane Fighting is the authoritative resource for mastering the Hooked Wooden Cane, Modern Tactical Combat Cane, Walking Sticks, Irish Fighting Shillelagh and the Bo Staff: 8.5 x 5.5, paperback, photos, illus, 242 pages.

MAXIMUM DAMAGE
Hidden Secrets Behind Brutal Fighting Combinations
by Sammy Franco

Maximum Damage teaches you the quickest ways to beat your opponent in the street by exploiting his physical and psychological reactions in a fight. Learn how to stay two steps ahead of your adversary by knowing exactly how he will react to your strikes before they are delivered. In this unique book, reality based self-defense expert Sammy Franco reveals his unique Probable Reaction Dynamic (PRD) fighting method. Probable reaction dynamics are both a scientific and comprehensive offensive strategy based on the positional theory of combat. Regardless of your style of fighting, PRD training will help you overpower your opponent by seamlessly integrating your strikes into brutal fighting combinations that are fast, ferocious and final! 8.5 x 5.5, paperback, 240 photos, illustrations, 238 pages.

SAVAGE STREET FIGHTING
A Tactical Savagery as a Last Resort
by Sammy Franco

In this revolutionary book, Sammy Franco reveals the science behind his most primal street fighting method. Savage Street Fighting is a brutal self-defense system specifically designed to teach the law-abiding citizen how to use "Tactical Savagery" when faced with the immediate threat of an unlawful deadly criminal attack. Savage Street Fighting is systematically engineered to protect you when there are no other self-defense options left! With over 300 photographs and detailed step-by- step instructions, Savage Street Fighting is a must-have book for anyone concerned about real world self-defense. Now is the time to learn how to unleash your inner beast! 8.5 x 5.5, paperback, 317 photos, illustrations, 232

THE BIGGER THEY ARE, THE HARDER THEY FALL
How to Fight a Bigger and Stronger Opponent
by Sammy Franco

Sammy Franco was concerned that no book on the market successfully tackled the specific problem of fighting a larger, stronger opponent. In The Bigger They Are, The Harder They Fall, he addresses that all-important issue and delivers the solid information you'll need to win a street fight when the odds seem stacked against you. In this one-of-a-kind book, Sammy Franco prepares you both mentally and physically for the fight of your life. Unless you're a lineman for the NFL, there may come a day when you will face an opponent who can dominate you through sheer mass and power. Read and study this book before that day comes. 8.5 x 5.5, paperback, photos, illus, 212 pages.

SURVIVAL WEAPONS
A User's Guide to the Best Self-Defense Weapons for Surviving Any Dangerous Situation
by Sammy Franco

Whether you are just commuting around town or preparing for a SHTF scenario, Survival Weapons: A User's Guide to the Best Self-Defense Weapons for Surviving Any Dangerous Situation teaches you how to choose with the most efficient weapons for any survival situation. A must-have book for anyone interested in real world survival and wants to dramatically improve their odds of prevailing in any high-risk combat situation. 8.5 x 5.5, paperback, photos, illus, 210 pages.

KNOCKOUT
The Ultimate Guide to Sucker Punching
by Sammy Franco

Knockout is a one-of-a-kind book designed to teach you the lost art and science of sucker punching for real-world self-defense situations. With over 150 detailed photographs, 244 pages and dozens of easy-to-follow instructions, Knockout has everything you need to master the devastating art of sucker punching. Whether you are a beginner or advanced, student or teacher, Knockout teaches you brutally effective skills, battle-tested techniques, and proven strategies to get you home alive and in one piece. 8.5 x 5.5,

CONTEMPORARY FIGHTING ARTS, LLC
"Real World Self-Defense Since 1989"
ContemporaryFightingArts.com

Made in the USA
Las Vegas, NV
21 November 2024

12307728R00118